TIME'S WITNESSES

Women's Voices from the Holocaust

Edited by Jakob Lothe

Photographs by Agnete Brun, Steve Nelson
and Jakob Lothe

Translated by Anne Marie Hagen

Fledgling Press Ltd, Edinburgh

First published by GYLDENDAL 2013
Copyright © Gyldendal Norsk Forlag AS 2013. [All rights reserved.]

This translation has been published with the financial support of NORLA

www.fledglingpress.co.uk
Printed and bound by: Ashford Colour Press Ltd
ISBN: 9781905916900

Preface

This book presents the histories of ten Jewish women who survived the Nazi concentration and extermination camps during World War Two. The women were born in Europe between 1925 and 1935. After the war four of them settled in Norway and became Norwegian citizens. Today, the six other women live on four different continents.

Time's Witnesses: Women's Voices from the Holocaust is inspired by *Time's Witnesses: Narratives from Auschwitz and Sachsenhausen* (2006), which I co-edited with Anette H. Storeide, and which presents the stories of eight Norwegian camp survivors. By focusing solely on these two camps, we were only able to find male survivors to interview. At the same time the necessity of communicating women's narratives became obvious. Working to present Norwegian women's voices from the Holocaust, it is a significant problem that none of the Jewish women and children who were deported from Norway to the Nazi concentration camps returned. This is the reason why the ten Jewish women who present their accounts in this book were born in other European countries.

Working on this book has been challenging. As these challenges concern both the way the book is structured and also are closely connected to the content of the narratives, I write more about this in the introduction. Yet I would also like to stress here that although the topic of the book is dispiriting, it has been a privilege to once again meet and listen to time witnesses who have put their confidence in me by telling me their histories. They also put that confidence in the readers of this book. Time and again I am struck by the strength and courage that these ten women demonstrate by thinking back on experiences they may rather want to put behind them in order to carry on with their lives. The irrepressible will to live which helped them survive is evident in the narratives. At the same time all ten women recognise that their survival depended on chance.

Nazi Germany's five-year occupation of Norway (1940–1945) was formative for the war generation. Parents and grandparents who were profoundly affected by their experiences during the war have also influenced those born after 1945. For my part, the greatest influence has come from my mother, Eldfrid Lothe. Mother was in Cambridge, England, when World War Two began in September 1939. She had a small black diary with the year '1939' printed on the cover. Reading her entry for 1 September 1939, detailing how shocked people in Cambridge were that Nazi Germany had invaded Poland, made an impression on me. For my mother the war became both formative and identity-confirming. And thus it became so for me as well.

***

I would like to thank Anette H. Storeide for the inspiration and good advice she has given me. I would also like to thank photographer Agnete Brun for her enthusiasm for this book project and for the portraits she has taken of the four Norwegian women, and photographer Steve Nelson, who has taken the portraits of Maria Segal and Judith Meisel. The portraits were taken at the time the witnesses narrated their accounts. I also thank the time witnesses for lending me the photographs taken of them when they were young and which are presented alongside the present-day portraits.

This book is not only inspired by *Time's Witnesses* (2006), but also by *After Testimony: The Ethics and Aesthetics of Holocaust Narrative for the Future*, a collection of essays which discusses how different forms of documentaries and fictional narratives can communicate, rework, and represent the historical event that was the Holocaust – and continue to do so after the last time witnesses are gone. I would like to thank my two co-editors of *After Testimony*, Susan Rubin Suleiman and James Phelan, and additionally, Jeremy Hawthorn, J. Hillis Miller, and Irene Kacandes, for their help and encouragement. I thank Janet Walker for inviting me to give guest lectures at the University of California, Santa Barbara, and for introducing me to Maria Segal and Judith Meisel, who both tell their stories in *Time's Witnesses: Women's Voices from the Holocaust*.

Several museums have been of help through their exhibitions and competent employees who have suggested time witnesses I could approach for interviews and who have assisted me in having the accounts adjusted and approved. I would like to thank The Jewish Federation of Santa Barbara, The Kaplan Centre for Jewish Studies (Cape Town), Sydney Jewish Museum, the Center for Studies of the Holocaust and Religious Minorities (Oslo), and The Jewish Museum in Oslo. Particular thanks go to Helga Arntzen, Marie Bonardelli, Jurina Boyes, Julie Feilberg, Richard Freedman, Marit Langmyr, Peter Major, Norman Seligman and Mariela Sztrum. Jane Arnfield,

Mandy Stewart, and Helena Svojsikova have been of great help with Zdenka Fantlová's account.

I thank Irene Levin for her valuable assistance as a consultant. Thanks also go to Oddvar Schjølberg, who gave me permission to use material from his book on Blanche Major, *Jeg overlevde Auschwitz* ['I survived Auschwitz'], and to Irene Engelstad, Per Kristian Sebak and Arne Johan Vetlesen for constructive comments on the introduction. Elin Toft and Anders Toft Lothe have given me invaluable help and support.

The most important task remains: to thank the ten survivors—the time witnesses who made this book possible.

Oslo, November 2016
Jakob Lothe

Introduction

The Norwegian Holocaust

During the autumn and winter of 1942–1943, 772 Jews were deported from Norway to the Nazi concentration and extermination camps, most of them to Auschwitz. Of these, 34 survived.

Of the Jews who were deported from Norway, *no* children and *no* women survived Auschwitz. For that reason, there are no witnesses for these two groups of Norwegian Jews. The approximately 300 women and children who were deported to Auschwitz were murdered. Here there is a narrative void—a silence. The situation in Norway thus differs completely from that in the other Scandinavian countries. As a neutral country, Sweden was not occupied by Nazi Germany, and the Swedish Jews were therefore not deported. In Denmark the Nazis attempted to deport the approximately 8,000 Jews, but thanks to large-scale civilian efforts, the vast majority managed to escape to safety in Sweden in October 1943. 481 Jews were arrested in Denmark and deported to the ghetto and the concentration camp of Theresienstadt—of these 52 died.

When Nazi Germany invaded Norway on 9 April 1940, about 2,100 Jews were living in the country. Their situation immediately became precarious. The historian Bjarte Bruland distinguishes between three phases in the Nazi hunt for the Jews in Norway. The first phase, from April 1940 to January 1942, was dominated by single actions that were not necessarily part of a systematic anti-Jewish policy. In a brief intermediate phase, from January to October 1942, preparations were made for the third phase: the extermination phase of October 1942 to February 1943. During this last phase the Norwegian police carried out a series of arrests of Norwegian Jews, and there were four deportations to concentration and extermination camps. The women and children were in the two largest groups, which were sent on the ships *Donau* and *Gotenland*.

The transport ship *Donau* sailed from Oslo on 26 November 1942, with 532 Jews on board. After several days at sea, the *Donau* arrived in Stettin, from where the Jews were transported in cattle trucks to Auschwitz. After their arrival on 1 December, they were subjected to a *Selektion*, with all women and girls, all boys under 15 or thereabouts, and all men over 45 being sent directly to the gas chamber.

The second major deportation of Norwegian men, women and children took place early in the morning of 25 February 1943. This time, 158 Norwegian Jews were deported on the transport ship *Gotenland*. From Stettin they were sent to Auschwitz via Berlin. They arrived in Auschwitz on 3 March. This time also, women and girls, boys under 15 or thereabouts, and men over approximately 45 were gassed immediately after the selection.

The void left by the Jewish women and children who were murdered in the Holocaust can never be filled. Even so, I view the accounts given by the 10 Jewish women in *Time's Witnesses: Women's Voices from the Holocaust* as not only bearing witness to the unimaginable number of people who lost their lives in this genocide but also as helping us not forget their Jewish fellow sisters and the children from Norway who also were gassed in Auschwitz.

A time witness has survived the Nazi prison camps and is thus able to bear witness to what actually happened in those concentration and extermination camps. There are not many time witnesses left now, and in a few years' time the last of them will be gone. More than half of the men who tell their story in the book I refer to in the preface, *Time's Witnesses: Narratives from Auschwitz and Sachsenhausen* (2006), are now dead. As yet, we do not know what the significance will be of no longer having time witnesses among us. However, I do not believe that the need for knowledge about the concentration camps and the Holocaust will diminish, but rather the contrary.

Approach

None of the women who were deported from Norway to Auschwitz in 1942–1943 returned. But four Jewish women who survived the Holocaust and who settled in Norway after the war have been willing to meet with me and tell me their stories: *Maria Gabrielsen, Blanche Major, Edith Notowicz* and *Isabella Wolf* have come forward as time witnesses in this book. As have six Jewish women who, like the Norwegian women, were all born in Europe, but who now live on four different continents: *Maria Segal* and *Judith Meisel* in the United States, *Yvonne Engelman* and *Olga Horak* in Sydney, *Ella Blumenthal* in Cape Town, and *Zdenka Fantlová* in London. I established contact with these ten women partly by approaching them directly; partly contact was made through introductions and help from the key persons I mention in the preface.

In addition to the Norwegian Jewish women I strongly wished to interview, I wanted to meet Jewish women who could tell me about the Holocaust from different perspectives in time and space. Since the Holocaust took place in Europe, it is not strange that many survivors wished to remove themselves from this part of the world. They spread out over large sections of the world, and the place from which they tell their story influences their narrative perspective. The variation in time perspective results from the fact that the women narrating were born between 1921 and 1935. The youngest, Maria Segal, was sent to the Warsaw ghetto when she was five years old, and her account is coloured by the fact that she experienced the deportation as a child. Similarly, the accounts given by Ella Blumenthal and Zdenka Fantlová are influenced by their having been about twenty years old when they were in the camps.

I have tried to maintain a balance between the need to give the book a unifying structure and the wish to control and influence the narrative situation as little as possible. With this as my starting point, I asked each of the time witnesses four questions, which I sent to them before our meeting:

1. Can you describe the circumstances that led up to your arrest?
2. Can you tell me how you experienced your imprisonment?
3. Can you say a little about your life after the war?
4. When you look back at your time in the prison camp, what do you feel it is particularly important not to forget, and what can we learn from what you and your fellow prisoners were subjected to?

Although I asked a few additional questions during the interviews, I mainly adopted the role of listener while the women narrated. The texts have been edited, but I have attempted to retain the narrator's tone and her own words and way of telling her story. As it differs how much a time witness wishes to and can manage to tell, these testimonies vary in length. The narrators are the authors of their own life histories and have all read the text, corrected errors, and approved their accounts.

In *Time's Witnesses* (2006) my co-editor, Anette H. Storeide, and I occasionally included the narrator's own reaction to what he was narrating—in square brackets. The reason why I chose not to do this in *Time's Witnesses: Women's Voices from the Holocaust* is that—in order to be consistent—I would have had to insert so many square brackets that the value of them would be limited. The narratives were often interrupted—sometimes by tears, but most often by a pause. On several occasions, the pause lasted so long that I was unsure if the narrator was capable of continuing. I have tried to retain something of these pauses by dividing the text into paragraphs. Even if it is perhaps difficult when reading, one can imagine a break in the narrative between the paragraphs. Closely linked to the pauses are the various forms of repetition. I have partially edited out these repetitions. Some, however, I have allowed to remain, because repetitions often convey meaning. It is a way of indicating that something is important—as when the time witnesses repeat how much they miss family members who did not survive.

In several instances a follow-up interview was scheduled. For example, having read the first draft, Ella Blumenthal felt that I had misunderstood so much that her interview simply could not be used as it was. But the most important reason for her not being able to approve the first draft was that she was dissatisfied with her own account. By telling her story to me, she had started to recall more of it—by narrating what she had experienced during the war, more was coming back to her. When she read my draft text, she did so from a different point of departure than the one she had during the first interview. This, combined with the formative experience of narrating, made a new version necessary. The other time witnesses, too, expressed the feeling that there was a distance between the oral and written versions of their accounts and made a few adjustments as a result, but none of them felt there was a discrepancy to the extent that Ella Blumenthal did. While some of the time witnesses have not previously published their story, others have published books and/or fairly short presentations (see 'Textual basis' and 'Literature'). This applies, for example, to Olga Horak, Maria Segal, and Zdenka Fantlová. However, the textual basis for their accounts in this book is not that which they have previously published but the interviews I recorded. I have nevertheless added a little information from the previously published sources. These additions have also been approved by the time witnesses.

A time witness who has previously written about her experiences will have processed the experiences in a different way from one who has not, and this can influence the oral account. There may also be a difference between time witnesses who have been, or still are, guides at museums or on organised educational trips to the former camps, and those who for various reasons have not been active in such work. I wanted the selection of narrators to reflect these variations. At the same time, the ten testimonies show that it does not necessarily become any easier for the survivor to tell her story of the Holocaust even if she has done so previously. The accounts of all the time witnesses are accompanied by periods of silence, and all are fragmentary and episodic in various ways. This does not make them qualitatively 'inferior', but rather the contrary.

The interview with Blanche Major in Oslo gave rise to special challenges and marked a boundary for what it is possible and what it is ethically defensible to do to get a time witness to give an account. Blanche Major suffered a stroke some time ago and almost completely lost the capacity to speak. This meant she was unable to tell her own story in the way the nine other women have done. But although she could no longer speak, Blanche Major was of sound mind, and since she distinctly expressed a wish for her story to be included in the book, I attached great importance to realising this. In 2009, Oddvar Schjølberg published *Jeg overlevde Auschwitz. Blanche Major forteller* ['I Survived Auschwitz: Blanche Major Tells Her Story']. Extracts from this book, which Schjølberg gave me permission to use, I combined with notes that Blanche Major's friend Marit Langmyr had taken during conversations with her prior to her stroke. I read the draft aloud for Blanche Major so that she could approve it sentence by sentence. Occasionally, she indicated that certain things had to be corrected. The new, adjusted version of the text was checked by her son, Peter Major, who had heard his mother tell of the Holocaust on many occasions. Blanche Major's powerful and unique story is a good illustration of the boundary or transition we are approaching—the point in time when time witnesses no longer can speak directly from this genocide. Blanche Major died in April 2014.

The contrast between evil and solicitude

As yet though, time witness are still able to speak—and they do so with a particular authority. Even though the Holocaust defies comprehension, we nevertheless understand more when we read or hear the story of a time witness. Their accounts remind us of the fact that the battle against Nazism and Nazi Germany was an ideological one, a battle of values that had to be won for Norway to be able to develop as a democracy. The political editor of the Norwegian newspaper *Aftenposten*, Harald Stanghelle, has rightly emphasised 'the importance of the time witnesses' powerful message of the collective active memory as a mental shield against future bestiality'. The accounts by these ten survivors bear witness to a bestial system that the Nazis developed 70 years ago. Although 70 years is a long time, it is really a short period, seen from a historical perspective.

The ethnic war was one of the strongest driving forces of the Holocaust—and this applies both to what lay behind this disaster and the implementation of the industrial mass murder of six million Jews. The hatred of the Jews was linked to the Nazis' conception of themselves as being qualitatively 'better' than them. It was also linked to evil or, more precisely, to evil human acts. The philosopher Arne Johan Vetlesen defines evil as 'to intentionally inflict pain and suffering on another human being, against her will, and causing serious and foreseeable harm to her'. In the case of the Holocaust, this was done systematically and industrially on a vast scale, but also individually and spontaneously. All the time witnesses in the book were exposed to different forms of evil. What is characteristic of all of these women is that they reacted just as strongly to the hatred and the evil acts perpetrated against others as to those acts they were personally exposed to. One example of this is Judith Meisel's description of how an SS soldier seizes a small child and dashes it to the ground, killing it. To Meisel, this spontaneous act of violence was not only hateful and evil but completely absurd. It symbolised that anything could happen.

It is meaningful to emphasise moral acts, as they are the diametric opposite of evil and as such contrast with, and express opposition to, the Holocaust. I am inspired by the Danish philosopher and theologian K.E. Løgstrup's idea that our dependence on the caring attitude and solicitude of other people is the distinctive characteristic that makes us human. The Nazi death camps were purged of all human solicitude, and this was one of the reasons why many prisoners felt they gradually became stunted as human beings. The prototype of the fundamental relation of moral solicitude is the relationship between mother and child—especially the newborn child, to which the mother first gives life and subsequently helps to live. Evil and solicitude are polar opposite moral actions that are both prominent in the accounts of the time witnesses. Even though the conditions in the camps were so bad that the prisoners had to struggle to survive from one day to the next, various forms of solicitude are nevertheless a striking feature of the accounts. The mother of the child that the SS soldier dashed to the ground and killed had done everything she could to protect it. In her account, Zdenka Fantlová tells of how she and the women she was with helped each other to survive the death march towards the end of the war. When they walked along side by side, they took turns to be in the middle. The woman in the middle was supported and held up by the women walking on either side, and in that way she was able to grab a few minutes' sleep.

Narratives—potential and limitation

Narratives surround us everywhere and at all times. One reason why the narrative is so crucial, is that, fundamentally, humans communicate and make sense of the world through narratives. A human life is like a narrative with a beginning, a middle, and an end, one where we like to see an inner coherence between the individual parts and a rationale for the choices we make. The ability to create and understand narratives is important for perceiving our human existence as meaningful.

Having said that, there is no narrative that can create meaning out of the Holocaust. Apart from the fact that it is difficult to narrate anything about hatred, evil, and loss, there are experiences that are so horrific that they cannot be narrated, or so extraordinary that they are beyond language, on which the narrative depends. In that sense, the accounts in this book have an element of defiance about them: they are narratives that resist the oppressors by using words instead of physical violence. The ten women's stories have the characteristics of testimony, which is a distinctive form of narrative. The dual dimension of acting as a witness illustrates the witness's often painful experience of being an onlooker and a participant at one and the same time. The survivors, via their testimony, bear witness to the atrocities to which they and others were exposed. At the same time, a witness is, in a profound sense, alone. From her lonely position the witness can point to an event and a dimension that goes beyond the witness herself. That applies to all the narratives in this book.

The former president of the Norwegian Parliament, Jo Benkow, who died on 18 May 2013, emphasised in the speech he gave on the international Holocaust Day on 27 January 2012 that the number of those killed in the Holocaust—around six million—'is so vast that it completely loses its human dimension'. He went on to say that during the war he had a cousin, Ada, who he was very fond of: 'I see her before me as she sat there, just out of the bath and wrapped in her mother's largest bath towel. She smelt sweetly of sunshine, as all newly bathed children do. She looked at me with bright eyes full of joy. There is a reason why I am telling you this. One cold day—I think it was 1 December 1942—she and the other female members of my family were stripped naked and crammed into a room the German racial hysterics called a shower. But no water came out—gas did. What took place there has haunted me the rest of my life.'

Jo Benkow shows how moving the narrative of a single individual is; at the same time he also manages to show how hard it is to tell Ada's story. He is left with a host of questions. Ada only lived to be four years old; she was one of over a million Jewish children murdered during the genocide.

While historians legitimise their presentations with the aid of empirical methods, the narratives of time witnesses are legitimised by having been personally experienced. A memory is not an exact imprint of the event in question, but it is formed in the context in which the person concerned finds herself when she tries to relate her experiences. In that way, memory is both selective and subjective: we ourselves choose what we want to—

and are able to—say about experienced events and relate them in the order and with the perspective, vocabulary, and emphasis we ourselves feel are right and possible. One might perhaps think that to bear witness to genocide is, from a moral perspective, simple, even though it inevitably is a tremendous physical and mental strain; the atrocities, that which the moral indignation is in reaction to, are in this case so vast and so obvious. Even so, it transpires that the time witnesses have to face difficult moral choices as regards their narratives, both when it comes to the choice of events and their presentation.

The Holocaust was a historical event. But there does not exist only one narrative of this event. As Zdenka Fantlová formulates it: 'Six million were murdered. If all of them had survived, there would have been six million different narratives.' Certain events in the camp were so monstrous and offensive that it can be difficult—and in certain cases morally indefensible—to relate them. One example of this is what Edith Notowicz says about Josef Mengele: the notorious doctor at Auschwitz 'had a special predilection for twins, but I can't go into details here. It is too horrible for me. He was also interested in finding new methods of sterilisation and thereby preventing the Jewish race from procreating. In the camp he had more than enough test subjects, and I was one of those who were used in Mengele's sterilisation experiments on Jewish girls.' Edith Notowicz displays courage in telling us as much as she does, and as readers we understand and respect the fact that she cannot 'go into details'.

Just as there is no 'correct' or 'complete' narrative of the Holocaust, there is no set answer to how much and in what way survivors are able to talk about it. As narrators, the time witnesses are continually faced with options: if they select one narrative variant, they deselect another. In difficult encounters with such choices they nevertheless manage to tell a great deal about what they experienced. It is precisely as an expression of subjective experience and memory that the time witnesses' narratives are so distinctive. They are not only important because of the facts they can communicate about what happened. The testimonies from the prison camps are particularly valuable because they testify to the actual witnessing process: they bear witness to the survival and to the resistance to death.

Between the portraits taken of the time witnesses at the time they told their stories to me and the photographs of them in their youth, there is a distance of roughly 70 years. A photograph is not a narrative, but there is a temporal dimension linked to it, lying on top of it, so to speak, as a visual expression of a person's life. For the viewer, it can contain elements of a narrative. If the person who sees the portrait of a woman then reads this woman's story, the narrative dimension in the portrait is enhanced. At the same time, the portrait gives the narrative a visual anchoring.

The act of narration is also enhanced through the combination of the portrait and the early photo. Since the time witnesses lost practically everything they possessed when they were deported, I was not only grateful but also surprised that all of them had an early photo to lend me; some of the time witnesses only had one photo of themselves taken before the war. While the early photos show the reader the women as they were during the period being referred to in their accounts, the portraits show them as they now are when speaking about that period.

As a listener, I was repeatedly struck by how soberly and credibly the time witnesses spoke of the difficult conditions under which they lived in the camps. This does not mean that all details necessarily are 'correct'. As the former Sachsenhausen prisoner Eskild Jensen says in his contribution to *Time's Witnesses* (2006): 'Memory is a somewhat unstable companion.' Many years have passed since these experiences took place, and like all other people the time witnesses can forget or remember incorrectly. Nevertheless, this is historical documentation: testimony from someone who was there and who literally experienced the concentration camp on her own body.

Tollef Larsson was imprisoned in two other concentration camps: Natzweiler and Dachau. In a conversation I had with him on 16 June 2013, he pointed out that the time witness, apart from being a witness in the ordinary sense, has been exposed to three mutually reinforcing experiences: dehumanisation, loss of identity, and encountering evil. It is the combination of these three experiences—experiences that extended over their entire time in the camp—which makes the time witness's narrative especially important, and which gives it its distinctive authority.

The European Holocaust

The American Holocaust Museum in Washington, D.C., defines the Holocaust as the systematised, state-financed genocide of about six million Jews carried out by Nazi Germany and its allies during World War Two. While the extermination of the Jews was the Nazis' main aim of the Holocaust, they also hunted down and killed a large number of non-Jews, including several thousand Roma, two million civilian Poles, almost three million Soviet prisoners of war, several thousand homosexuals and Jehovah's Witnesses, many thousand political prisoners of war, and 200,000 handicapped persons. The Nazis deported Jews from large parts of Europe—from Tromsø in the north to Rhodes in the south-east, from the British Channel Islands in the west to villages deep inside the Soviet Union in the east.

Recent research has revealed that the extent of the system of camps and ghettos was much larger than we were previously aware of. Behind such well-known names as Auschwitz and the Warsaw ghetto there was a network of smaller sub-camps and bases—42,000 in all, where Jews were systematically hunted down, arrested, incarcerated, and murdered. (This information and the following overview of camps such as those the ten time witnesses survived has mainly been taken from *The United States Holocaust Museum Encyclopedia of Camps and Ghettos, 1933–1945*.) The women who tell their story in this book were at several of the largest camps and also at several of the lesser known ones. The conditions in the small camps were also terrible. The whole camp system was characterised by brutality towards the prisoners, frightful, unhygienic conditions that often led to disease, and food that was both insufficient in terms of amounts and which had little nutritional value.

The Warsaw ghetto

Two of the time witnesses in the book, Maria Segal and Ella Blumenthal, were sent with their families to the Warsaw ghetto, the largest of all the Jewish ghettos established by the Nazis during the war. The ghetto was surrounded by a three-metre-high wall, and after the ghetto was sealed off on 16 November 1940, anyone attempting to escape risked being shot on the spot. Within an area of less than three per cent of the total area of Warsaw, the Nazis crammed over 400,000 Jews from the city and the surrounding area. They made up 30% of the population of Warsaw.

Like other ghettos in Poland, including that in Łódź, the Nazis organised the administration of the ghetto via a *Judenrat*. In the Warsaw ghetto this Jewish council was led by Adam Czerniaków, who chose to collaborate with the Germans. When he, in 1942, realised that collaboration was futile, he took his own life. The conditions in the ghetto were wretched. In 1941 the Jews' daily food ration contained less than 200 calories, while that of the ethnic Poles was 700, and that of the Germans, 2,600. It was exceptionally difficult to find work in the ghetto, and the lack of food gradually grew critical.

By the summer of 1942, over 100,000 Jews had died in the ghetto from various diseases or from starvation. Then the Nazis started to deport Jews from a rounding-up point in the ghetto, the *Umschlagplatz*, to camps which, after the invasion of the Soviet Union on 22 June 1941, had been established in the eastern part of Poland. Most of them, 265,000 Jews, were sent to the extermination camp of Treblinka in the period from 22 July to 12 September 1942. After a pause of about four months the deportations were to start up again in January 1943. This time, however, the Germans met resistance from a group of Jews who had managed to procure weapons.

On 19 April 1943, which was the day the Jewish Passover began that year, the German forces started the operation to annihilate the ghetto. However, when they entered the ghetto that morning, the streets were empty. Then the Jewish Combat Organisation, *Żydowska Organizacja Bojowa* (ŻOB), under the leadership of Mordecai Anielewicz, launched an attack on the German forces and forced them back onto the other side of the ghetto wall. After three days, the SS returned with reinforcements and started to blow up one building after another, so as to force the remaining Jews to surrender. Mordecai Anielewicz was killed when the SS, on 8 May, seized the ŻOB's commando bunker at 18 Mila Street. In spite of this, some individuals and small groups of Jews continued to fight the German forces. To mark the fact that all resistance was over, the Nazis blew up the large synagogue on Tlomackie Street on 16 May 1943. By that time, the ghetto had been virtually razed to the ground. The revolt in the Warsaw ghetto was the largest and, symbolically speaking, the most important Jewish revolt in German-occupied Europe. Even though the uprising was suppressed, there were few deportations in the following couple of months. This revolt was also an inspiration for the armed revolts in the Treblinka extermination camp on 2 August 1943 and in the Sobibór extermination camp on 14 October 1943.

Majdanek

In connection with the revolt in the Warsaw ghetto more than 50,000 Jews were killed. Almost all the approximately 40,000 Jews still alive in the ghetto were deported to the concentration camp of Majdanek and to various labour camps. Ella Blumenthal was among those sent to Majdanek.

Majdanek was under construction nearly the entire time the camp existed. The first prisoners were Soviet prisoners of war, who arrived at Majdanek in October 1941. Most of them were too weak to work, and by February 1942 nearly all of them were dead. The first Jews to be deported to the camp had been arrested on the street in Lublin or fetched out from the Jewish ghetto in the town. Later, Jews arrived from other camps, including Czech Jews from Theresienstadt. When Bełżec was to be closed, in autumn 1942, about 25,000 Jews were transferred from that extermination camp to Majdanek. It is unclear if they were killed on arrival or registered as prisoners, but after six months there was practically no one left of the Bełżec transfers.

When the surviving Jews from the revolt in the Warsaw ghetto arrived in Majdanek in the spring of 1943, the great majority of the camp prisoners were Jews. Many of the arrivals from Warsaw who were too weak to work were killed with toxic gas. Later that same year Majdanek was the scene of one of the most frightful individual events of the Holocaust, *Aktion Erntefest* (Operation Harvest Festival). *Erntefest* was the code name for the massacre in which 18,000 Jews were shot on 3 November 1943. Half of the victims were from Majdanek; the others had been fetched from various labour camps in the Lublin area. During the massacre, loud music was played over the loudspeaker system in Majdanek to drown out the noise of the shootings. In terms of the number of people killed, this was the largest massacre carried out on a single day during the Holocaust. (The largest number of murders during a single 24-hour period took place on 29–30 September 1941, when 33,771 Jews were executed in Babij Jar near Kiev.) After *Erntefest* there were only a few Jews left in Majdanek. When Soviet forces approached the camp in July 1944, it was evacuated so fast that most of the camp was intact when the Red Army moved in on 24 July. Majdanek was the first major concentration camp to be liberated.

The Kovno ghetto and Stutthof

Judith Meisel was among the Jews who were sent to the concentration camp Stutthof in July 1944 from ghettos and labour camps in the Baltic area. She arrived at Stutthof from the Kovno ghetto in the city of Kaunas (Kovno), which was at that time the capital of Lithuania. When the Soviet Union invaded Lithuania in June 1940, Kaunas was one of the cities in Europe with the largest population of Jews. About 40,000 (a quarter of the inhabitants) were Jews. Kaunas was a Jewish centre of education with several schools, and there were 40 synagogues in the city. Though conditions for the Jews had become more difficult after the Soviet invasion, they were to get much worse when Nazi Germany invaded Lithuania just over a year later. Prior to the Germans closing in on Kaunas, the pro-Nazi mob had already killed several hundred Jews. In early July 1941 the German *Einsatztruppen* started systematic massacres of Jews in the forts that the Russian tsars had built around the city. Before the year was over, the Germans had murdered half the Jews in Kaunas.

The remaining Jews were squeezed into a small area in the city district of Slobodka. One difference from the Warsaw ghetto was that the prisoners of the Kovno ghetto were forced to do various kinds of work in factories and businesses outside the ghetto. Inspired by the Warsaw revolt, there were several resistance groups in the Kovno ghetto. The Jews also documented the conditions via secret archival material (notes, diaries, photographs) which they hid in the ground and which was found by the Russians after they had liberated the ghetto on 1 August 1944. By then the Nazis had blown up the ghetto using grenades and dynamite, and most of the remaining prisoners had been deported to camps further west.

In 1944 the Nazis started using the gas Zyklon B to kill off prisoners who were too weak to work. Under brutal conditions, the prisoners were used as forced labour in the armaments industry, including the Focke-Wulff airplane factory. Stutthof was constantly being enlarged and finally had 105 sub-camps. Over 60,000 prisoners died at Stutthof.

Under pressure from the Soviet forces that were approaching from the east, the evacuation of Stutthof began in January 1945. At that time there were about 50,000 prisoners in the camp, the vast majority of whom were Jews. 5,000 prisoners were marched down to the Baltic coast, forced out into the water and machine-gunned to death. In late April 1945 the remaining prisoners were evacuated by sea, as Stutthof was now completely surrounded by Soviet forces. The risk of being torpedoed by Soviet submarines was considerable that late in the war. On 16 April the transport ship *Goya* (built at the Akers mekaniske Verksted shipyard in Oslo in 1940) was torpedoed near the Bay of Danzig, which resulted in more than 7,000 refugees drowning. The ship on which Judith Meisel was travelling was also torpedoed. When the Red Army liberated Stutthof on 9 May 1945, Russian soldiers found about 100 prisoners who had been able to hide away during the evacuation.

Theresienstadt (Terezín)

Maria Gabrielsen and Zdenka Fantlová were both deported to the ghetto and transit camp Theresienstadt, which lay close to the small town of Terezín in the northern part of what is now the Czech Republic. The town was established in the 18th century as a fortress town and named after Queen Maria Theresa of Austria. Theresienstadt, which existed from November 1941 to May 1945, was a combination of ghetto, transit camp, and concentration camp. A total of about 140,000 Jews were deported to this ghetto. Of these, almost 90,000 were 'sent eastwards', as Zdenka Fantlová expresses it. Practically all of these were murdered at Auschwitz, Treblinka or Majdanek. As the expression 'sent eastwards' indicates, those in the ghetto had no idea what awaited those who were deported. But when no one returned, people gradually started to fear the worst.

Maria Gabrielsen and her siblings were among the 15,000 children who were in Theresienstadt for either a longer or shorter period of time. Many of the children wrote poems and drew pictures—a selection of the drawings is exhibited at the Jewish Museum in Prague. Considering that almost 90% of the children perished, it is quite exceptional that Maria Gabrielsen and all her six siblings survived.

Apart from the psychological stress that was triggered by the overhanging risk of being sent on, the conditions in the ghetto itself were miserable. The death rate was so high that the Nazis in 1942 built a crematorium just south of the ghetto. Yet Theresienstadt had a rich cultural life created by artists, musicians, and actors who, before the war, had helped to make Prague one of Europe's most important cities of culture.

The Nazis exploited the cultural life of the ghetto for propaganda purposes. This culminated during the visit they allowed the International Red Cross to make to Theresienstadt in June 1944. Prior to the visit, the Nazis intensified the deportations from the ghetto so that it would not appear to be overcrowded. The prisoners were ordered to plant flowers and paint the buildings, and the representatives from the International Red Cross were invited to several cultural events. Furthermore, the Nazis forced the German film director Kurt Gerron (also a well-known actor who had starred alongside Marlene Dietrich in the film *The Blue Angel* from 1930) to make a propaganda film with the title *Der Führer schenkt den Juden eine Stadt (The Führer Gives a City to the Jews)* to demonstrate how 'humane' the conditions at Theresienstadt were. Upon completion of the film, Gerron and his wife were sent with the last transportation to Auschwitz and murdered on arrival.

When Theresienstadt was liberated by Soviet forces on 8 May 1945, SS Commandant Karl Rahm and the last of the Nazis had fled just a few days earlier. While Zdenka Fantlová by then had experienced the liberation of Bergen-Belsen, Maria Gabrielsen and her siblings were, a few weeks after the liberation, sent by train from Theresienstadt back to Vienna. Among the few musicians to survive was the pianist Alice Herz-Sommer, who gave more than 100 concerts in Theresienstadt. Alice Herz-Sommer, who was born in Prague in 1903, subsequently lived in London, as did Zdenka Fantlová. Until her death in February 2014, Alice Herz-Sommer was the oldest known survivor of the Holocaust anywhere in the world.

Auschwitz

Zdenka Fantlová was among those 'sent eastwards' from Theresienstadt to Auschwitz. Blanche Major, Edith Notowicz, Yvonne Engelman, Olga Horak, and Ella Blumenthal were also deported to Auschwitz, the largest of the Nazi concentration and extermination camps.

The building of the camp started in summer 1940 in the Polish town of Oświęcim, which in German was given the name of Auschwitz, 60 kilometres west of Kraków. Two important factors that had significant impact on the development of Auschwitz were the war against the Soviet Union, and the German industrial concern IG Farben, which established a factory adjoining the camp. Over the first years of the camp's existence, the camp area was steadily expanded, and from late 1943 onwards it consisted of three independent camp areas: Auschwitz-I (the original concentration camp and main camp), Auschwitz II-Birkenau (extermination camp), and Auschwitz-III-Monowitz (labour camp for IG Farben) as well as more than 40 satellite camps. The best-known commandant at the main camp, Rudolf Höss, had begun his career at the concentration camp of Sachsenhausen before coming to Auschwitz.

Auschwitz-I was established in a former military barracks in the early summer of 1940. By 1943 the number of prisoners had mushroomed to about 20,000. The first prisoners were Polish political prisoners. Gradually, prisoners arrived from many countries, and both Soviet prisoners of war, Roma and Jews were victims of systematic extermination; most of them were killed in the gas chambers of Birkenau shortly after arrival. Birkenau, which was built during the autumn and winter of 1941–1942, lay about three kilometres from the main camp. This camp was the scene of the largest Nazi mass murder of Jews and Roma. Birkenau consisted of various sub-camps where, for example, Jews from Theresienstadt and Roma were kept separate from each other. The camp normally housed around 100,000 prisoners.

Most of the prisoners that came to Auschwitz were killed shortly after arrival. Able-bodied men in their twenties and thirties, however, had a chance of survival since they could be exploited as forced labour. It was mainly at Auschwitz-III-Monowitz that prisoners carried out such work. Auschwitz-III was established for the German industrial company IG Farben in 1941, and here the company built a factory called *Buna Werke* for the production of synthetic rubber. This camp normally had around 10,000 prisoners.

In early September 1941 the first killings using the gas Zyklon B took place in a holding cell at Auschwitz I. Because the killing capacity was too small, a gas chamber was later built in the camp crematorium. When the capacity at Auschwitz I was outstripped by numbers once more, a building at Birkenau was converted for use as a gas chamber in January 1942, and a further building was converted that same summer. After this initial phase in which provisional gas chambers were improvised in this manner, permanent buildings were erected and equipped for the specific purpose of mass murder, and Jews from all of Europe were deported eastwards to be killed. At the Wannsee Conference on 20 January 1942, the problem of organising the mass murder of European Jews was discussed, and 1942 was also the year when the preparation and erection of the death factory at Auschwitz took place. Unlike the extermination camps of Bełżec, Sobibór, and Treblinka, a considerable amount of forced labour took place at Auschwitz. But Birkenau was expanded into an extermination machine.

In 1942, two large and two smaller crematoriums with gas chambers were built; they became operational in 1943. This radically increased the killing capacity at Birkenau, and in 1943 the industrial extermination of Jews and Roma began in earnest. In spring 1943 Doctor Josef Mengele arrived at the camp. Medical experiments such as sterilisation had also taken place before his arrival, but Mengele additionally started a series of new experiments, including the notorious experiments on twins. He was also responsible for selecting prisoners for the gas chambers. The purpose of the 'selections' was to find able-bodied prisoners who could be used for forced labour. But even for those so categorised, the inhuman conditions led to many dying.

In May 1944 the extermination process at Birkenau was streamlined by extending the railway lines all the way into the camp. At the same time the ramp where the selections took place was moved from a branch line outside the camp to the camp area itself, only 100 metres from the nearest crematorium-gas chamber complex. These changes were linked to the major deportations from Hungary in the spring and summer of 1944. During this period the killing machinery at Birkenau was operating at its most intensive pace. The photograph of the main gate into Birkenau and the railway lines ending at the selection ramp is today one of the most powerful and well-known images of the Holocaust.

1944 marks the year the largest number of prisoners were killed at the camp as well as a year of chaos and collapse. In August 1944 Monowitz was bombed by the Americans and badly damaged, but not destroyed. Towards the end of 1944 the SS started to dismantle the gas chambers in their attempt to eradicate all traces of the atrocities committed at the camp.

Towards the end of the war Auschwitz was evacuated and the prisoners sent on death marches westwards and southwards. Tens of thousands of already exhausted and sick prisoners died during these marches or were shot because they were unable to go any further. In the winter of 1945 some of the survivors arrived in various concentration and labour camps such as Gross-Rosen and Kurzbach before some of them finally ended up at Bergen-Belsen.

On 27 January 1945 Auschwitz was liberated by the Red Army. At that point there were more than 1,000 survivors at the main camp, more than 6,000 at Birkenau, and about 600 at Monowitz. The Auschwitz complex was the largest Nazi camp complex, both in terms of geographical extent, the number of prisoners, and the number of prisoners killed. About 70% of the prisoners were killed shortly after arriving at the camp. This applied, as mentioned, to the Norwegian children, the Norwegian women, and the Norwegian men over about 45 who came to the camp in the autumn of 1942 and winter of 1943. The exact number of deaths at Auschwitz is uncertain, because those who were murdered upon arrival were never registered as prisoners.

Two trials were held to seek justice for the crimes committed at Auschwitz. Most of the key personnel of high rank, including camp commandant Rudolf Höss, were first called to testify as witnesses in the Nuremberg trials, after which they were transferred to Poland, where they were put on trial in 1947. The majority were given the death sentence, and Höss was hanged in front of the crematorium at Auschwitz the same year. The gallows remains in place today as part of the war memorial. The trials at Frankfurt am Main in 1963–1965 are referred to as the second Auschwitz trial. This is the largest trial on participation in the genocide of European Jews. While the Nuremberg trials focused on the best-known Nazi figures, the 22 accused in the second Auschwitz trial were guards of lower and mid-level rank and lower and mid-level camp administration officials. In the course of the four-year preparation period more than 1,300 depositions were collected, and during the actual trials 359 people from 19 nations appeared as witnesses. When the sentences were passed in August 1965, they gave rise to international dismay because of the relatively short sentences and some acquittals.

Auschwitz stands as a symbol of the Nazis' mass extermination of humans they believed did not have a right to life. Auschwitz is also the camp that most people associate with the Holocaust. There are a number of potential reasons for this. The most important one is probably that Auschwitz is the Nazi camp where the most people were murdered: a total of 1.1 to 1.3 million people were killed at the camp, most of them ending their lives in the gas chambers.

Since the Auschwitz complex was also a camp where prisoners were used as forced labour, some prisoners had a chance (although very slim) of survival. They were therefore able to keep memories of the camp alive and later testify as to what had taken place there. This contrasts with Bełzec, Sobibór, and Treblinka, where practically no one survived. As a result, 'single-purpose' extermination camps have acquired a much smaller place in our memories of the Holocaust even though, as a percentage, more people were killed there than at Auschwitz. As a symbol, Auschwitz represents more than what took place in that camp. Horrific acts of violence took place both before and after Auschwitz. But, as the writer Laurence Rees writes in his conclusion to the book *Auschwitz*: 'We must judge behaviour based on the time at which it took place. And judged from the middle of the 20th century and the sophisticated European culture of the time, Auschwitz and the Nazi 'Endlösung' represent the basest act in all history.'

Labour camps

In spring 1944 Isabella Wolf saw the Jews at the reception camp in Hungary where she was being held be brutally divided into two groups: while one group was deported to Auschwitz, she ended up in the group that was sent to the labour camp of Heiligenkreuz in Austria. In August 1944 Blanche Major, who was among the many Hungarian Jews deported to Auschwitz in spring and summer 1944, was sent from Auschwitz to the labour camp of Stadtallendorf, west of Berlin. In October of the same year, Edith Notowicz, along with 350 Hungarian Jewish women, was sent from Auschwitz to a labour camp in the town of Hainichen, whilst Olga Horak and Zdenka Fantlová had to undertake forced labour near the town of Kurzbach during the final winter of the war.

The distinction between a concentration and a labour camp was a fluid one in the network of camps that the Nazis established in order to implement the Holocaust. The labour camps were for forced labour, and many of them are referred to as KZ camps (concentration camps). A common feature of the labour camps was that the prisoners received too little food in relation to the hard physical work that they had to carry out. This imbalance, one that led to many prisoners dying, was a planned consequence of an overall guiding principle for the entire system of concentration and labour camps in Nazi Germany: *Vernichtung durch Arbeit* (extermination through work). Much of the forced labour during the last winter of the war was carried out for the German armaments industry.

Apart from the inadequate food, the prisoners wore thin and inappropriate work clothing, and they lived under terrible, unhygienic conditions and were treated brutally by the guards. Even so, work conditions varied quite a lot from camp to camp. There could also be considerable variation within an individual camp: particularly in winter there was a big difference between being ordered to work outdoors and working indoors. Other factors which impacted on the overall conditions were the person in command of the prisoners, and the other prisoners they worked alongside. One thing that often proved decisive at all labour camps was whether the prisoner managed to stay healthy, or if he or she fell ill. A prisoner incapable of working was not worth much in the brutal camp system. Accounts from the labour camps also contain striking examples of the care and solicitude the prisoners could show one another, even in the highly pressured situation in which they found themselves.

Bergen-Belsen

Olga Horak, Ella Blumenthal, and Zdenka Fantlová were among the prisoners from Auschwitz who ended up at Bergen-Belsen. They shared the same fate as many thousands of other prisoners who were sent to this concentration camp as the Nazis evacuated the camps further to the east before fleeing from the Red Army.

Bergen-Belsen was established in 1940 just north of the town of Celle, and until 1943 it was solely a camp for prisoners of war. It then became part of the concentration camp system and was really a complex of camps with various categories of prisoners: Jews, prisoners of war, political prisoners, Roma, 'asocial individuals', criminals, homosexuals, and Jehovah's Witnesses. In addition, Bergen-Belsen became a reception camp for prisoners who came from camps further to the east, so that the number of prisoners rose from approximately 7,000 in July 1944 to 22,000 in February 1945 and 60,000 when the camp was liberated on 15 April 1945. In parallel, food rations gradually decreased, and from January 1945 onwards the prisoners had to do without food for days on end. There was also a lack of fresh water. This combination led to a violent increase in deaths resulting from disease—particularly typhus, but also from TB and dysentery.

When the British forces liberated the camp, they were met by a dreadful stench. Many thousands of dead prisoners had not been buried. A film team from the BBC accompanied the British forces. The film made by this team about the conditions in Bergen-Belsen shocked Western Europe and North America and is considered one of the most important films in the history of documentaries. Altogether, about 50,000 prisoners died at Bergen-Belsen. A further 13,000 former prisoners were so ill that they died shortly after the liberation. The British established a camp at Bergen-Belsen for displaced persons—former prisoners who no longer had a home after the war.

In autumn 1945 a British military tribunal put 48 SS staff from Bergen-Belsen on trial. They were charged on the basis of guidelines for the treatment of prisoners of war laid down in the Geneva Convention of 1929. Eleven of the accused, including the camp commandant Josef Kramer, were sentenced to death, as was the notorious prison guard Irma Grese, who, before she came to Bergen-Belsen, had worked at Ravensbrück and Auschwitz.

Survival strategies—silence and narrative

We tend to think of a narrative as something that follows on from silence, and also that silence and narratives are opposites. When it comes to the narratives in *Time's Witnesses: Women's Voices from the Holocaust*, things are not necessarily that simple. Just as there are many forms of narrative, there are many forms of silence. Even though the narrative act is active, all forms of silence are not *per se* passive. Just as the narrative is a strategy for survival, so can silence be. Both these human activities are complex and become even more so when we look at them in connection with each other— which we can hardly avoid doing when it comes to the narratives in this book. There is also a difference between the silence of the victim and that of the perpetrator of the suffering the victim has undergone. A third variant of silence is that which the historian Raul Hilberg refers to as *bystanders*—those who cannot or will not talk about what they saw, and who could perhaps have done more to prevent it. Considering that there were 42,000 camps, stations, and rounding-up points for Jews, there must have been many bystanders in Europe in the twelve years Hitler was in power.

By the term 'survival strategies', I am thinking particularly of various strategies that the time witnesses used, more or less consciously, to go on living after the war. But the women also had to have survival strategies in the camps—strategies for surviving from one day to the next. Admittedly, the time witnesses point out how little they could change things and how much everything depended on good fortune, on sheer luck. But this also meant that it was crucial to choose and act correctly in the situations where this was possible, such as finding the right place in the queue for food, for example. Even though it is a question of different forms of survival strategies, there are points of intersection between strategies for survival in prison camps and strategies to enable one to live on as a free individual afterwards.

The women who tell of the Holocaust try to find words for events that are so horrific that they evade language. The narrative is a strong form of communication that can take the narrator back to the events she is talking about. This can prove problematic if what she first and foremost needs to do is to put these events behind her and get on with life.

There is no answer sheet for what is right or wrong when it comes to staying silent or speaking out about terrible events and traumatic experiences such as genocide; what may be a good strategy for one survivor may not necessarily be so for another. While many time witnesses remained silent for the rest of their lives, it is characteristic of the accounts in this book that the relation between silence and narrative is more a *both/and* than an *either/or* situation.

Silence precedes and succeeds the time witnesses' narratives. For most of the time witnesses a period of more than 50 years passed before they started to talk about their experiences. When they now narrate, the account constantly takes them to a point where the act of narration comes to a halt. A pause occurs, which is a form of silence. The Holocaust researcher Irene Levin writes in her article 'The Speech of Silence': 'There are always certain silent stories whose voices we will never hear. But if we listen precisely to the silence between the words, the silence in the actual story itself, sometimes a chance opens up of extending our knowledge and understanding.' As Irene Levin also writes, one 'cannot interview people about their silence. The silence does not exist for them.' It is not certain that the women experienced the time from when they survived the camps up to the point, many years later, when they were able to start to tell of their experiences as being one of imposed silence. Perhaps the question of silence or narration was irrelevant to their survival strategy during this period. But now it is important for the ten time witnesses to narrate.

If the time witnesses start to narrate after a period of silence, they also communicate their stories approaching the demarcation line that will be drawn by their own passing. Looked at from that angle, the space of time for the testimony is short—something the women clearly demonstrate they are very well aware of. This form of time-concentration—between the ending of the silence and the ending of the possibility of narrating—helps to give the narratives a distinctive intensity characterised by moral gravity.

Narratives by women are under-represented

Since there are so few female time witnesses who can speak from direct experience about the Holocaust, both in Europe in general and in Norway in particular, their accounts have been under-represented and, to a certain extent, underrated. A narrative that is not realised through words is difficult to comprehend. Silence is easily overlooked. From this perspective the testimonies of the time witnesses in this book are particularly important. By telling their stories, the ten women can stir up unpleasant thoughts and be reminded of losses against which they have used silence to protect themselves. The act of narration thus demonstrates courage and will-power.

The fact that there can be different forms of courage can be another reason why women's narratives are under-represented in the literature about the Holocaust and World War Two. Not all forms of courage are equally visible. While, for example, Ella Blumenthal showed courage taking part in the revolt in the Warsaw ghetto, the testimonies in the book document that courage can also be displayed without the use of weapons and must not be overlooked even though it is a form of courage not expressed in words. This is where silence once more enters the picture. One example is the mother of the baby that the SS soldier dashed to the ground and killed. Judith Meisel says that the mother afterwards refused to open one of her hands—she was clenching something she did not want to reveal. When the soldiers finally got the mother to open her hand, they saw a baby's shoe. The SS soldier ordered her to hand it over. When the mother refused, she was shot. This mother is one of the heroes of the Holocaust: a hero with moral integrity who not only showed great love of her child but also impressive courage.

Both female and male time witnesses experienced dehumanisation and loss of identity, and they encountered evil. At the same time, *Time's Witnesses: Women's Voices from the Holocaust* shows that there were events at the camps which women experienced differently from men. To have to strip naked in front of male SS officers is not the same for a woman as for a man. Several of the women relate how terrible it was to have all body hair removed: they experienced it as being deprived of part of their female identity. There are also differences in the way women and men experienced Josef Mengele's medical experiments; in *Time's Witnesses* (2006) Julius Paltiel talks about such experiments in a more direct way than Edith Notowicz is able to do here. Many women were raped, not only by German soldiers and civilians but also by Russians and other men on the side of the Allies. One of the greatest differences was that the women were together with their children at the camps. They had to experience their children being murdered, or starving to death.

Concentration camp prisoners of both sexes showed care and solicitude for each other. Samuel Steinmann, for example, showed great solicitude for his brother at Auschwitz. During the death march from Auschwitz to Gleiwitz in January 1945, Julius Paltiel and Samuel Steinmann saved Leo Eitinger's life. The latter later became a prominent Norwegian psychiatrist. At the same time it is striking how strong caring relations can be for women and between women in the narratives in *Time's Witnesses: Women's Voices from the Holocaust*. This applies, for example, to the care shown between Olga Horak and her mother, between Edith Notowicz and her friend Ilona, and between Maria Gabrielsen and her siblings. And it also applies to the mother who held on to the shoe of her murdered child. It is as if the care they show each other forms a moral defence against all the evil they see around them. That such caring is less visible and surrounded by less noise than physical fighting may have contributed to there being fewer narratives about women's caring *for* others in extreme war situations than we have narratives about men's fighting *against* others in similar situations.

Narrating so as not to forget

The time witnesses who relate their stories in this book are not historians, and their approach is, and must be, different. They were there. They experienced imprisonment. They survived imprisonment. And they have gone on living with the memories from their imprisonment. Now they are to talk about what they experienced about 70 years earlier. It was a world of starvation, cold, disease, death, abuse, suppression, humiliation, and fear. There are experiences that the time witnesses no longer recall; there are episodes and events they are uncertain about. But they were there, and they want to talk about what they remember, such as they remember it, so that posterity will not forget it. Because the time witnesses tell us their stories, we also gain insight into what happens when human rights, love of one's fellow human beings, and respect for human life are ignored. As long as we have time witnesses among us who are able to communicate their stories, as the ten women in this book do, the Holocaust is close to us.

By not forgetting we increase the possibility of not repeating and not passively accepting hatred and evil deeds carried out against our fellow human beings. If we seek to forget or downplay such attitudes and deeds, the time witnesses are there as a sharp reminder of the great risk we run if we do not take their message to heart.

Maria Gabrielsen

Born on 3 January 1934. Deported to Theresienstadt in 1943, where she remained until the end of the war. Lives in Sandefjord, Norway.

I remember being four years old well. We lived at home in Vienna then. We were seven siblings, and we had a good life. Dad was a tailor and worked from home. He used a treadle sewing machine to make suits, and he had customers he supplied. He had a large clothes iron with a lid. Into that he put glowing pieces of coal from the stove. It hissed when he ironed the clothes he had moistened. This fascinated a little girl, and it was from Dad I inherited my interest in sewing.

Dad was Jewish, and his name was Michael Schwarz. Mum's name was Rosa, and she was of German descent. She had converted from Catholicism to Judaism. We lived in a flat in the Simmering district. One day a man suddenly came running out into the hallway where we children were playing. He was holding a baby in his arms, and he shouted: 'It's war! It's war!' He was completely disturbed and tossed the baby into the air. This was the first time I'd heard the word 'war'. I wondered what it was.

From 1938 onwards our situation dramatically worsened. German soldiers marched into Austria on 12 March 1938, and conditions quickly became much more difficult for the Jews. Dad lost his customers, food became scarcer, and we had to start using ration cards. The cards were green with red letters. They showed that we were Jews, and if we dropped a card on the ground and had to bend down to pick it up, we were spat on by those who stood around us.

Mum was very strict. She often shut us in the flat. If one of us had done something she believed was wrong, everyone got a beating with the carpet beater, which hung from a hook by the door so that it was easy to get hold of.

I started school when I was six years old. In the classroom we had to sing for Hitler; there was a picture of him on the wall behind where the teacher was sitting. We also had to pray to Hitler, for he gave us our daily bread. I thought that was strange. At home we had not seen much of the bread from Hitler, and I had realised that Dad did not like him. So I didn't either. Dad found work in the coal mines; I think it was in Poland. Once in a while he came home to visit, and that made us very happy.

Gradually, most things became forbidden for the Jews. All sorts of injunctions were imposed. We could not ride the tram any more and were not even allowed to go to the cinema. We were told that anywhere dogs were not permitted, Jews were not allowed to enter either.

Mother fell in love with an SS man. We children were never allowed to see him; we always had to be outside when he came to visit. One time Dad came home, Mum didn't want to let him into the flat. One of my older sisters, Berta, gave Dad some clothes, and then he went to a friend's place to stay the night. What Mum did then, was to report her husband to the Gestapo. Dad was a Jew, so they were already looking for him and were of course happy to have her help. Then he was taken and sent to a labour camp in Vienna.

Next, Mother reported my three eldest siblings—Erwin, Hilda and Berta. They were taken straight away and ended up in the labour camp as well. Now she was busy getting divorced, and soon she didn't want anything to do with her four youngest children either. As she was of German descent, she had good help getting the 'Jew brats' out of the flat.

Two ladies came and collected the four of us and took us to a children's home. This time we were allowed on the tram, but we had to stand at the exit. We barely had clothes on—just a dress, no underwear or shoes. We didn't bring anything with us either, for Mother had sold a lot of what we had at home.

It was a children's home run by Jews. They took good care of us here— we were allowed to bathe and were given clean clothes. We were divided by age group, girls and boys separately. We had to help out with various tasks.

We were not allowed to go to school, but the 'aunts', as we called them, tried to teach us a little. We learned how to say bedtime prayers, and I still do.

Sometimes uniformed Germans with guns came. When that happened, we had to stay completely quiet and not say a word. There was a courtyard at the children's home, and one day when we were outside playing, two Germans came and said that if we made that much noise, they would shoot us all. We were terrified, and the adults understood that this could have been intended seriously. After that day there was no more outdoor play in the afternoons; only a few children were allowed outside at a time to get some air.

After a while we learned that Dad and our three oldest siblings had found a small flat in Zirkusgasse, not far from the children's home. We were allowed to visit them on Sundays, and that was nice. But we had to wear a Star of David badge. At first the star was pinned to our jackets, and we would take it off as soon as we had passed through the gate. To prevent us from doing that, the star was sewn on by machine. Whenever we met kids in the street and they saw the star, they would throw rocks at us, pull our hair and spit at us. We were not allowed to fight back. On the street where our dad and siblings lived, there were so many ruffians that we were scared to walk there. But we squared our shoulders because we wanted to visit them, of course.

We were comfortable in the children's home. The 'aunts' and 'uncles' treated us with respect. When it was somebody's birthday, the birthday boy or girl was allowed to sit at the head of the table, and they wrote whose birthday it was on the blackboard. Events like that were highlights in our lives. We were particularly fond of 'Uncle Fritz' and 'Aunt Ditta'. We were thrilled when we, after the war, found out that they were both among the few adult survivors from the children's home, and that they, on top of that, had married each other. But both Fritz and Ditta's parents were sent to Auschwitz and murdered there.

While we were in the children's home, dramatic things were happening at home which we only found out about later. Dad and my three eldest siblings were still living in Zirkusgasse. But the SS man Mum was seeing died after eight months. Shortly afterwards she entered into a new relationship, this time with a fervent Nazi called Mathias Schnedlitz. They fell in love and wanted to marry as soon as possible, but to do that, Dad first had to sign the divorce papers. When Dad refused, Mum went to the Gestapo offices and reported her husband to the Nazis. She told them that not only was Michael Schwartz a Jew, he was also a communist who opposed the Nazis. Mum had become an informer who betrayed her husband after 20 years of marriage.

Dad was arrested immediately. This was in April 1942. He had to endure long interrogations in the Gestapo headquarters in Vienna, and then he was convicted of anti-Nazi activity. He was put in a labour camp for a few weeks, and then he was sent to Auschwitz. He was murdered there in the autumn of 1943.

When Mum found out that Dad was dead, she asked to have the death certificate sent from Auschwitz. As soon as she had that, she married Mathias Schnedlitz. But Mum did not stop at this. She went to the Gestapo offices again and reported her three eldest children, Erwin, Hilda and Berta. They were quickly apprehended and sent to a forced labour camp outside Vienna.

In the children's home we had no idea about this. Nobody told us that Dad was dead or that our eldest siblings had been sent to do forced labour. We arrived at the children's home in 1941. In April 1943 I was admitted to hospital, probably with measles. But one day I was suddenly fetched back to the children's home. When I arrived, I noticed that the mood had changed. I saw a few girls who were leaning over the banister in silence. It was as if the air was charged with uncertainty. I was smartened up and taken up to the sewing room. There I discovered that my bag had been packed and was lying on the table, with my name written on it in black letters. That's when I realised that we would be sent away now.

It's as if my childhood ends here. Not long after, I met my three other siblings, and suddenly Erwin, Hilda and Berta were there too. All seven siblings were together again, but in a sad and difficult situation. Each of us was handed food and clothing in a bag from the children's home. A truck was waiting outside, and we were heaved onto it. People who were standing around the truck gave us a little food. Perhaps they felt sorry for us.

We were driven to the railway station. There were a lot of people there, and uniformed Germans with their dogs. We were ushered on board the train—the carriages had wooden benches for sitting. Then the train began to move. We had no idea where we were going. The train frequently stopped, and when that happened, German soldiers walked through the carriages to make sure that everything was in order. I didn't like the sound of their boots; it's a sound I [still] associate with something painful.

The train ride lasted a long time—I cannot remember exactly how long. It was dark by the time we arrived at a loading ramp. One of the soldiers entered our carriage and shouted *Raus!* We were to get out, all of us, and leave all luggage behind. So I had to leave my bag with my few possessions behind. On the platform we were then examined by the Nazis and by Czech police officers. They checked whether we had any jewellery or money or other valuables. Everyone who had gold teeth was registered. From me they took my one earring. It was so beautiful, with a little red heart, and I only had this single one left. It was a great sorrow, losing that earring.

On the platform we were divided into two groups: women and children under the age of twelve were to be taken to one barracks, while boys and men over twelve were to be taken to another. Erwin was 21 years old and ended up in the group with the adult men. We girls and our little brother Kurt, who was six, were allowed to stay together. Then we were escorted into a large barracks. People in striped clothes were leaning against the fence watching us. Some people in our group tried to talk to them but were brusquely told to stop. In the barracks we had to take off all our clothes, as everything had to be disinfected. I had no idea what disinfection was, but I later understood that the Germans did this because they were terrified that they'd get lice.

Then we were showered and all our hair cut off. I was distraught when one of the prison guards cut my hair with clippers. My long black locks disappeared, and now I looked just as strange as the other prisoners. I hoped that I would get my clothes back, but instead we had to pull items out of a big pile of clothes to see if we could find something that fitted us. Everything had to be done so fast. *Schnell! Schnell!* they yelled. 'Quickly, quickly!'

That first night we were put in a large dormitory. There were bunk beds with a mattress, a pillow stuffed with straw, and a blanket. I was together with my siblings, apart from my oldest brother, who I didn't see again. I was tired from the train ride and fell asleep pretty quickly. That was my first night in Theresienstadt.

The next morning, we were able to see the camp in daylight. We saw blocks encircled by fences. Above the gate was the slogan *Arbeit macht frei* ('Work sets you free'). The youngest four of us stayed together; the eldest were sent to another barracks. All the adults had to work whereas we were sent to a sort of children's home where we were divided by age. Jewish inmates looked after us. They came from various countries. The first things we were given were a tin can that sort of resembled a tin of Norwegian fish balls, and an aluminium spoon. We had to take care of these, we were told. But none of the things we had to hand over were returned to us. Afterwards we found out that whatever was usable in our luggage was sent to Germany.

In the mornings we had to take our tin and fetch coffee, which was sort of like brown water. It was boiled, and we were not to drink the water from the tap. We didn't have any kind of toiletries. There was water and a trough where you were supposed to wash in cold tap water.

We had to wait in a long queue to get food. Every now and then children collapsed from exhaustion. When that happened, someone usually came to pull them out of the queue. It was usually pea soup for dinner. It was made from dried yellow split peas. There were a lot of maggots in that soup, but they floated to the top when the soup had come to the boil. We removed the maggots and continued eating. Every other day we were given a piece of bread. We were supposed to save this so that it lasted for two days. The bread was teeming with maggots, and they were alive. We learned to pick out some of the maggots using our fingers. After all, we had to have food.

In the straw-filled bunk beds there were a lot of fleas and bedbugs. We could be itching terribly at night when we were trying to sleep. They bit, and to mute the pain, we scratched until we bled. Then we got lice, which are very contagious. They made our scalps itch. Apparently, they lay their eggs behind the ear, where it is warm. The lice were a pain. When they crawled across your body, it felt as if your skin was moving.

There was no school in the camp, and teaching was not allowed. But some of the adult Jews who looked after us managed to get hold of some pencils and a few pieces of paper, and they came up with activities with educational elements. They were inventive: for example, the geography teaching was in the form of guessing games. We managed to soak up a few things. Someone always kept watch by the door, and when the Germans came riding up on horses to inspect us, the lookout let us know straight away. When the Germans entered the room, we sat completely quiet. That could be nerve-racking.

A lot of people were burned in Theresienstadt. They died, and then they were burned. The smoke from the crematorium had a sweetish smell. Every day the guards walked around the camp with two-wheeled flat carts. They tossed the dead onto the cart like sacks of flour and wheeled them to the crematorium. The ashes were placed in boxes. Several of the kids had to stand in a row and heft the boxes of ashes onto a truck. The boxes were all the same size so that they could be neatly stacked on the truck. You couldn't ask what they were going to use the ashes for—you wouldn't get a reply anyway. But for the work we could have a piece of bread, or perhaps even a piece of sausage. Oh, that tasted very good.

In the autumn we kids had to pick chestnuts. The chestnut trees were outside the barracks where the Germans lived. We had to pick up the chestnuts from the ground and put them in sacks. When there was snow, we had to dig through the snow to find the chestnuts. It was cold, and we were freezing because we didn't have proper footwear. That has been a problem for me ever since—my legs itch when it is cold.

Then there was a period when I received an injection every other day. I was terrified each time. I don't know what it was, but I think it must have been some kind of experiment. The fear of syringes stayed with me for a long time afterwards. I contracted tuberculosis, but nothing was done about that until after the war. I was terribly thin, but then we all were. And so time passed. We would be at the children's home in Theresienstadt for close to two years.

There was a cinema room in the camp where we would sometimes be assembled. Uniformed Germans sat in the stands while we girls sat on wooden benches. After having examined us closely, they pointed at some of us: 'You' and 'you' and 'you' were to step aside—and we never saw them again. I was lucky; they skipped me. This happened several times.

There was a blind girl in the camp children's home. I grew very fond of her. She was a very good singer, but her hands were so ugly and wrinkly. I couldn't help myself and asked why. 'They poured boiling water over them,' she said. I felt even more sorry for her then and sat down close beside her. She was so happy and sang for me. She had such a lovely voice. Her name was Erika. But then she was selected in the cinema, and I never saw her again.

Transports arrived carrying sick prisoners from other camps. They arrived in cattle trucks, and many of them had typhus. That was very contagious. When a transport arrived, the prisoners were ordered to jump down from the carriage. Many were so weak that they simply fell down. They wore next to no clothing. Between the train station and the camp there was a stream. The prisoners were told to jump across the stream because they were going to be counted. Those who couldn't manage, and many couldn't, were pushed into the stream. Then the Jews had to pull them from the water, and they were taken to the camp crematorium. We could see this clearly from the window in our barracks.

It was the prisoners who had to move the dead to the crematorium. Several times a day we could see them collect people who had died. They had a pull cart with two wheels and heaved the bodies onto that. One prisoner pulled the shafts at the front; another walked behind and pushed. The prisoners with the cart had regular rounds to pick up the dead.

In the spring of 1945 we noticed that the Germans were under pressure. The soldiers and officers were clearly unconfident, and rumours were rampant. One of the rumours said that the Danish Jews were going to be returned to Denmark. This was a nerve-racking time. What would the Nazis do to us? Perhaps they would kill us before they fled? The trains departing from the camp were now packed with Germans leaving Theresienstadt. We later heard that the Germans had decided that we were for the gas chamber on 8 and 9 May. Jews were forced to build it. The gas chamber was almost finished, but the Germans had not received Zyklon B.

Then we were lucky enough to be liberated. After a while we heard gunfire and the roar of canons—it lasted for two days. On 8 May, at two in the morning, the Russians arrived with tanks and trucks. The aunts in the children's home entered the room shouting: 'The war is over!' We wondered what that meant. The Russians threw food and cigarettes from the trucks. Many were so malnourished that they couldn't handle the food.

Shortly afterwards the first White Buses entered the camp. Two days later the first buses left, heading for Denmark with cheering Jews on board. Uniformed nurses gave them food and treated them with kindness. This was completely new and unfamiliar to us, who were used to sharp commands. I remember the red crosses on the roofs of the buses very well, as I could see those from the window. Remaining there behind the barbed wire fence was hard.

At first we were not allowed to leave the barracks. It was dangerous because people were completely wild, and several people were trampled to death fighting to get food. Then we were told that we could look for our families in the camp. It turned out that all my siblings had survived. It was incredible! There was nothing I rather wanted than to be with them. An aunt from Yugoslavia wanted to bring me home with her. I began to cry because I was so scared that I would lose my siblings. The aunt said she understood and that it was fine.

All seven siblings travelled together back to Vienna. It was a long journey, and we brought nothing with us. We arrived at a children's home where they received women and children from the concentration camps. We were given food and shelter there.

We all had a burning wish to meet Dad. We had no idea what had happened to him. It was only after we had arrived in Vienna that we heard that Mum had reported Dad and that he had been murdered in Auschwitz. That way Mum had obtained a death certificate for Dad so that she could marry her new boyfriend. It beggars belief that Mum could do this to her husband and her children. To this day, I cannot understand.

The papers wrote about us, for it was very unusual that all the children in a Jewish family survived Theresienstadt. Then something outrageous happened. As the children's home had been bombed, there was no water. My two youngest siblings went to collect drinking water because we were about to eat dinner. On the way back they had sat down on some steps next to a cinema to have a short rest. That's when my youngest brother, Kurt, sees a lady walking back and forth, and Kurt says to Annie, my sister: 'But isn't that Mum?' The lady hears his question and walks up to them. She asks what their names are, and then she says: 'Don't you want to come home with me? I've saved food and clothes for you now.'

I was on my way downstairs to eat and met my siblings and this lady on the stairs. I did not see who she was, and Annie asked me: 'Can't you see that it's Mum?' I looked up and straight into her blue eyes—she had blue eyes, the rest of us had brown eyes and dark hair—and I almost had a stroke. I flew down the stairs, I was so frightened! I hid in a bombed-out temple. I stayed there for many hours. Berta and Grete hid as well; they didn't want to see her.

Mum demanded her three youngest children – Kurt, Annie and Maria. Hilda, my eldest sister, said: 'You can't have them.' Hilda notified the manageress of the children's home. And the manageress reported Mum to the police. Mum was arrested not long afterwards.

It took time before Mum's case was brought before the court. A while after she had been arrested, we left the children's home. Hilda had received help from the City Council to find a small flat, and the youngest of us children lived there for a while. Then we were placed in foster families. I was placed with the Höger family. I was eleven years old and needed care and security. But this family had only taken me into their home for the pay they received from the Council. They exploited me—I even had to darn stockings!—and they practically regarded me as a necessary evil. I wasn't even allowed to eat with them but had to wait in the hallway. When they were finished, I was allowed to eat the leftovers before I had to do the dishes and tidy up. I simply had to do what they told me to. I was, after all, used to that.

One day I was so down that I went into the kitchen and turned the gas on. I wanted to end it. But then I started thinking about my siblings—how much I loved them and how sad they would be. I turned the gas off and opened the kitchen window wide. It was a close thing.

Mum's trial shocked Austria. She had probably not considered the possibility that any of her seven children would survive Theresienstadt. When we then suddenly turned up, we became the prosecution's strongest evidence. During the trial in Vienna it emerged that it was Mum who had turned in her three eldest children to the Nazi authorities. She denied this, but the evidence was damning. Brazenly, she also expressed that she felt deeply distressed when she was notified by the police of her husband's death in Auschwitz. But a married couple in the apartment building we lived in told the court that one day she had been in their flat, Mum had said that she had to 'get rid of the Jew' now. And according to another witness, Mum had told her that she wanted to divorce her husband because he was a Jew.

Of us children, only Erwin and Hilda attended the trial. They could testify about what Mum had done to Dad and to us. They wanted to shield us, the youngest, and did not tell us anything. It was not until 2004 that I saw the transcript from the trial. That was grisly reading. The verdict was passed on

24 June 1947. Even though Mum pleaded not guilty, she was found guilty on all counts and sentenced to five years' hard labour for having violated her children's and husband's human rights. She was also convicted of having contributed to her husband, Michael Schwartz, being deported to Auschwitz.

Five years after Mum was released in 1952, she attempted to claim compensation for war damages because she had lost her husband in Auschwitz. Her claim was dismissed by the court. We had no contact with Mum following her conviction. She died in Vienna in 1972, 83 years old.

When I had been with the Höger family for one and a half years, we were going to go on a school trip. I had to go to the doctor for a check-up. Mrs Höger wanted me to go to her doctor, but I wanted to go the doctor who had treated me before. It was a long walk to his office; I didn't have money for the tram. This doctor's name was Otto Wolken. He was also a Jew and had been at Auschwitz, but he was one of the survivors. Doctor Wolken was so kind; he respected me and listened to me. He discovered that I had contracted tuberculosis in the camp and that I was not well when I lived with the Höger family. Then he told me that I would get a trip to Norway with one of my siblings. We would be there for one month to be fed well and grow stronger. I only weighed 34 kilos. Then Doctor Wolken asks: 'Who is the thinner of Annie and Kurt?' 'Both,' said I. 'Well, then we'll have to try to send all three of you,' he said.

Within 14 days we were ready to leave. I was excited and ecstatic for the opportunity to get away from the family who only exploited me. We were told about Norway—that there was a lot of water and that we would have to use a boat to go from one house to the next. And that people wore costumes and wooden clogs. We were told all sorts of strange things. In July the travel papers were sorted, and we arrived in Oslo by boat on 3 August 1947. We were surprised to see that flags were flying from all the buildings. I thought the flags were for us, but then we were told that it was because it was King Haakon's birthday!

Altogether there were 60 Austrian children on this holiday to Norway. I was going to Elverum and my two siblings to Hamar. They were sent to a family with no children, who kindly welcomed them and later adopted them. I was sent to the Nordholm family, who had a farm at Øksna, north of Elverum. I will never forget the meeting with Oline and Ingvald Nordholm. I was received with open arms—they greeted me with warmth and love. I was given a piece of pink dress fabric with a bicycle print and in addition a shoe box with chocolates that the eldest son, Johan, had bought in Sweden. I will never forget this gift.

Oline and Ingvald understood that I had had many painful experiences, and whenever these memories intruded, they were there to comfort me. They were all so kind, their children and the neighbours who came to visit too. I was allowed to go with them to the pastry shop, and there I had cream cake! I'd never had that, and it tasted delicious. Every time we went to Elverum we visited a pastry shop and ate cream cake. Gradually, I began to feel safe. Luckily, it turned out that we three siblings were allowed to stay in Norway not just for one month, but permanently.

When I was thirteen years old, my foster parents moved to Larvik to lease a large farm. We were there for four years. I went to Rødbøl school. This was a pleasant time, and I found many new and good friends. I was also confirmed there. After I had finished school at Rødbøl, the family moved back to Elverum where I was accepted at the domestic science college. But after a while I decided to return to the Larvik area. My three foster brothers were leasing a farm in Kjølling by Larvik where they were growing vegetables. I wanted to give something back to my foster family and helped them with various things around the house. I stayed there for three years. The day I received my certificate of Norwegian citizenship, 26 November 1954, was a big day for me.

That same year I got to know Asbjørn Gabrielsen from Larvik. I felt very safe with him, and soon we both understood that there was something more than ordinary friendship between us. We have been married for 56 years now. We built a house just outside of Sandefjord in 1963 and have lived here ever since. We have two children, three grandchildren and three great-grandchildren. They make me grateful and are a great joy.

My siblings spread out across the world. Annie, Kurt and I stayed in Norway, while Berta settled in Israel. Erwin moved to Australia just after the war, but Hilda chose to remain in Vienna. Grete also went to Australia and worked there for 13 years before she and her husband settled in the USA. Today it is just Grete, Annie and I who are still alive.

I have always enjoyed working with my hands. I worked with vegetables for ten years, then I went to vocational college for my catering and hospitality qualification, and afterwards I worked as a cook in a kindergarten in Sandefjord for twelve years. When the kindergarten closed down, I enrolled in a folk high school and retrained again, and found work in a care home for the elderly. I enjoyed that too—I like to work with both children and with old people.

In 2004 I received a compensation of 36,000 Norwegian kroner from Germany—not from Austria. It was such a small sum that I thought it was ridiculous. In connection with the compensation payment, I received a request for an interview. I was persuaded to accept, and after the interview had been printed I was contacted by the founder of *Aktive Fredsreiser* [Travel for Peace], Helga Arntzen. Helga asked if I wanted to join *Aktive Fredsreiser* as a time witness on a trip they were arranging.

The first trip was horrible. We first arrived at Theresienstadt. The tour leader asked if I recognised it. 'I'm missing the railway tracks,' I said. Then they suddenly popped up. I then said: 'I'm missing another thing. I'm missing the stream.' I had no sooner finished speaking than the stream popped up. That's when I started shuddering. Sure enough, that was the way it used to be. We were going to walk through a subterranean tunnel in the camp, but I couldn't. All the time I felt as if someone was grabbing me. It was awful.

The next stop on the trip was Auschwitz. That was also terribly difficult. This was where Dad had been deported to. He had been here for five months before he was murdered in one of the gas chambers. I got this information from a Catholic priest I met in Auschwitz, by the way. He was very friendly, and he asked me if I wanted him to search for Dad's name in the archive. I wanted that very much, and he found out that Dad had been on four different work details. His health failed, and he was sent to the gas chamber.

There have been further trips to Auschwitz as a time witness. I go there with young people. I tell them that they have to do everything in their power to prevent the Holocaust from being repeated. Young people are the key—they are the ones who will lead Norway in the future. I tell them, now you've seen the scene of the mass murder of the Jews, and I see that Auschwitz makes an impression on them. I get a lot of good feedback from the young people I tell my story to. Once I overheard someone who was denying that the Holocaust ever took place. Usually I don't interfere in other people's conversations. But this time I could not help myself—I went over there and told them who I was and what I had experienced. That silenced him.

For many years after the war I had a difficult relationship with Germans. But then one summer when we were out in our boat, a German boat anchored next to ours. I didn't want to speak to the Germans on board and hid in the cabin while Asbjørn was on deck chatting with them. His German wasn't quite up to it, so he called to me. Even though I didn't want to, I thought I had better go out there. And they were so pleasant! It was a younger German couple, a husband and wife with two children. We invited them to our home, and we are still friends. They live in Bremen, and we have visited them there and have got to know several of their friends.

It is important not to forget, but I can't go around thinking about my stay in the camp all the time. There were so many painful experiences—there were so many who were beaten and whipped, and so many who died. They cannot be returned to us. But we can relate our story, tell what really happened, and warn against the destructive power of hatred. The Holocaust has consequences for our future. We must never be indifferent to the abuse that is committed today. Indifference is the ally of evil.

Soon all those who survived the Nazis' atrocities will be gone. In the new and demanding situation that will arise then, more people might come to deny the Holocaust. That's when young people, including those I have been to Auschwitz with, must be ready to protest.

Ella Blumenthal

Born in Warsaw on 15 August 1921. Deported to the Warsaw ghetto in October 1940. Deported to Majdanek in 1943, then to Auschwitz and then to Bergen-Belsen, where she remained until the liberation of the camp on 15 April 1945. Lives in Cape Town.

In spite of surviving the Warsaw ghetto and three death camps, after the liberation I tried to integrate into a normal society, and after I had married, I raised and educated my four children. But I wasn't able to talk about my suffering and fight for survival, because the open wounds were still bleeding.

I was born in Warsaw, the youngest in a family of seven children. My father was a respected and well-to-do textile merchant. My mother and siblings were engaged in the family business. I was a happy teenager until the Germans invaded Poland on 1 September 1939.

After weeks of heavy air raids, the city of Warsaw also fell. There was panic, uncertainty and fear, particularly for Jews. New orders and declarations were coming out daily. All Jewish land was requisitioned; all Jewish bank accounts were closed, blocked. All public gatherings were forbidden; all Jewish schools and synagogues were closed. Food was rationed. Curfew was imposed. We had to wear white armbands with a blue star on the sleeve of the outer garment. We had to hand over our radios. Jewish men were caught in the streets to do forced labour.

My father was also one of them. Since the synagogues were closed, daily prayers were held in private homes. He was caught in the street coming back from the prayers. When he came back home, we could not recognize him. His clothes were covered in mud, the collar was ripped out of his coat. Half of his beard was cut off. When he came back from work, he announced that he now realized that we are in the hands of murderers. Some men who did not report to work were shot.

Around this time I fell ill and was running a very high temperature. All infectious diseases had to be reported to the authorities. But there was a problem: the sick person who was sent to hospital never came back alive. The family was sent to be quarantined, where really they got sick. The home was fumigated, and before it was sealed all precious items were stolen.

In October 1940 we were herded into the ghetto. We managed to collect some of our belongings into sheets—like clothing, bedding, and some valuables. We did not forget our Torah, which my father managed to save from his synagogue. The rest of our possessions were looted by the Poles.

The ghetto was surrounded by high walls with barbed wire and broken glass on top. There were refugees pouring in from surrounding towns and villages, escorted by German guards. The ghetto was overcrowded. There were 10 to 15 people living in a room.

There was malnutrition, starvation, epidemics and disease. Starving children in rags were begging in the streets: 'Give me a piece of bread, or a couple of *Groschen*. I haven't eaten for days.'

A common sight every morning was corpses laid out during the night by the families of the deceased. Victims of starvation and typhus, they were covered with newspapers held down by bricks.

It was impossible to survive on the food rations, and therefore smuggling of food was rife in the ghetto. Food sold at exorbitant prices, and only those who could afford it, bought it. Some smugglers managed to get food in by bribing the guards at the gate of the ghetto. There were also little boys, the stronger ones, with bodies so thin that they managed to squeeze through the cracks in the walls of the ghetto. They got over to the other side where the Christian Poles lived. Sometimes they could be carrying their mother's wedding ring to trade for food, or they were just begging for food. But on their way back they were often caught. At best, they were beaten up after having been shaken so that the provisions fell out from under their clothing. But most often they were shot, and one could see their little bodies hanging

44

over the wall or lying on the ground in a pool of blood. They were our first ghetto fighters, and we salute their memory.

There were also some Jewish men who worked in German workshops outside the ghetto and who sometimes managed to smuggle in some food on their way back home. There were also Polish policemen who smuggled food into the ghetto and sold it at exorbitant prices. And some of our people brought out their last belongings in order to buy some food for their starving families.

The raids and round-ups of Jews continued in the ghetto. Streets were cordoned off, and anybody who was caught in the closed-off areas was deported. The raids even extended to flats. And it didn't matter whether it was young people, mothers with babies, children or old people; everybody was dragged down the stairs while pleading. Entire families vanished. To make it easier for themselves, the Germans announced that anybody who would voluntarily report to work would be given three pounds of bread and jam. There was no shortage of volunteers. But when these people did not come back, we realized that what we thought were only rumours, unfortunately must be true.

At the same time our underground organization was printing leaflets. This is one of them:

Citizens, Jews, awaken from your lethargy: stand up to fight. Do not believe that they are sending us to labour camps. It is a vicious lie. Our brothers and sisters are being brutally murdered in the death camp Treblinka. Brothers, prepare to defend yourselves. Those who are not fit for fighting should go underground and hide in cellars and bunkers. Turn every building into a fortress. We have no right to occupy the surface of the earth, because we are condemned to death.

It was hard to believe that such atrocities were happening. But I was one of those who did believe what the fliers said, and I left my workplace, which was called *Wertefassung*: our job was to collect and register all valuable items like paintings, artworks, tapestries, and antiques that were left in the flats by people who were deported. We loaded these items onto trucks which were sent to Germany. I left *Wertefassung* with a few of my friends, and we went underground while moving from cellar to cellar to avoid being caught. We became known as the 'wild ones', as we were unknown to the authorities and had lost our ration cards.

One of the orders our family was given was to hand in all our silver. We also had to give up our furs; they were sent to the German army on the Eastern Front. Due to the constant and frequent raids, the population of the ghetto was shrinking. The Germans were gradually reducing the size of the ghetto. And so it was with my own family: it grew smaller and smaller. I lost practically my entire family. Due to a miraculous chain of events there were three of us left: my father, my eldest niece Roma, and I. The rest of the family of 22 people were all deported. The three of us, together with a few of my young friends, occupied a flat in the building of Mila 19; the owners had been deported. Mila 19 was opposite Mila 18, which was the headquarters of the ghetto resistance movement.

We immediately set to work and bricked up the doorway leading to the last room and placed a heavy mahogany wardrobe in front to camouflage the brickwork. One could not tell there was another room in the flat. When we walked up the stairs to the next floor, the flat above was laid out exactly like ours below. We found a spot leading down to our bricked-up room. We cut out a square in the parquet floor, broke through the ceiling, and lowered ourselves on a stepladder into our room below. The last person pulled a broken cot over the opening before closing the hatch. We sat in this bricked-up room every day, venturing out only at night. At this stage, the Germans didn't come into the ghetto at night. As we sat there, we could hear them marching in every morning shouting orders, looking for Jews. We even heard their heavy footsteps on our staircase and, once, even in the adjoining room. They shouted: *Wo sind die verflucthte Juden!* ('Where are the cursed Jews!')

With us in hiding was a young couple with a baby. The mother had to cover the child's face with a pillow in case it cried out.

In 1943 Passover began on an evening in April. I remember my father giving everybody a piece of Matza[—the unleavened flatbread which is an important element in this religious festival—]which he had saved from the previous year. After reciting the prayers, he prayed to God to save us like He freed the Jews from slavery in Egypt. When the Germans marched in for their routine raids the next morning, they were met with Molotov cocktails, homemade bombs, grenades, and shooting from windows and rooftops. The Warsaw ghetto uprising had started. The Germans were taken by surprise, and they withdrew, leaving behind their dead and injured. Yes, German blood was flowing in the streets of the Warsaw ghetto. The next morning they came back with reinforcements and a tank. But they came up against young men and women who would not give up, and the fighting went on and on. But unfortunately, in the end they could not stand up to the mighty, well-equipped German army, and the uprising was crushed.

In retaliation the Germans decided to fetch every living Jew out of the ghetto. But by then we were all already hiding underground in cellars and bunkers. The only way the Germans could manage to achieve this was to smoke us out. So they decided to set the ghetto on fire, building by building. We had to leave our bricked-up room because the building was on fire. We got down the burning staircase and the gate that was on fire, made our way through other burning buildings, and came back to the last courtyard of our own building on Mila 19. Only this courtyard was intact.

Earlier, we had prepared a much safer bunker in this very courtyard. We dug beneath the cellar floor to make a bunker. Here we stored some provisions like dried bread, spaghetti, water, candles and horse fat, all of which we obtained with great difficulty. But we had to have it to sustain ourselves. We could only sit or lie in the bunker because the ceiling of the cellar was very low. Every night we climbed out to get some fresh air and straighten our limbs.

But then one night it became unbearably hot. We couldn't breathe; we were suffocating. We realized that this building was also on fire now. We had to climb out. When we got out of the bunker, it was as bright as day even though it was night. The whole ghetto was on fire. The scarlet flames were reaching towards the skies. The smell of the burning feathers from the bedding is forever in my nostrils. And the sight of the burning ghetto will never leave me.

There were people running around with their clothes on fire, with their hair singed and their skin scorched. Others were jumping out from their hiding places, and their bodies caught on balcony rails, where they were left hanging. I saw a woman sitting on a step with a baby sucking at her breast. I shook her, and somebody pulled me away saying, 'Can't you see that she is dead?'

Informants ran around urging us to get out of the inferno. These informants, and there were Jews among them, were promised by the Germans that they would not be deported if they found Jews in hiding. But eventually they met that exact same fate. The informers said, 'Yes, there are Germans outside in the street, but you won't be deported or shot. You will be resettled to the East where you will work with your family in the German workshops.' Instead of being burned alive, many followed these prompts. But when they got out into the street, they were immediately rounded up and deported.

But we, our small group that had kept together in all of the bunkers, we rebelled. And even in this dark hour when we were trapped with nowhere to turn, we still resisted and refused to submit. Remember the couple with the baby who were hiding with us? We called the man Moshe Baker. Before the war, he owned a bakery in the courtyard of Mila 19. He pointed out a spot below ground where he used to keep flour, and we lowered ourselves into that narrow place. We stood there, so tightly pressed together that we couldn't move our limbs. Every night we used to climb out to get fresh air and straighten our limbs.

But one morning we heard heavy footsteps above us and a rifle butt knocking on the trapdoor. *Raus, raus, verfluchte Jude!* 'If you don't come out, we will send gas down.'

We realized that we had been betrayed and that we had no option but to climb out. Outside we were blinded by daylight, which we hadn't seen for long weeks, living underground. And then we were ordered to stand with our hands above our heads, facing the courtyard wall. We waited to be shot. I prayed to G–d that I should be shot first, before my father, who was standing next to me, and before Roma, who was standing on the other side of my father. But we were only searched for weapons, as they knew that we Jews were armed. And then we were ordered to place all our valuables into a sack which was placed in the middle of the courtyard. Then we were chased into the street, where the buildings of our ghetto were still smouldering.

Already three weeks had passed since the heroic uprising began, and I believe that we were among the very last survivors holding out underground in the bunkers under the burned-out Warsaw ghetto. We were marched to *Umschlagplatz*. This was a place of no return. *Umschlagplatz* was a rounding-up point at a railway siding where the cattle trucks were packed to capacity with human cargo. They returned empty, ready for another load.

As the train was not there yet, we had to wait on the floor of an empty hall in an adjoining building. When it got dark, Ukrainian and Latvian guards in black uniforms stormed in and pulled out young girls. My father managed to cover Roma and I with his long coat.

I remember that when we were ordered down to the platform the next morning, my father gave a lump of sugar to an old man who was walking in front of him. When we reached the platform, the old man was motioned out of the line and shot, almost at our feet. He was too old to even make his last journey. And then we were chased into the trucks. *Schnell, schnell!* And those who couldn't run fast enough were hit with the whips and rifle butts. We were forced into the cattle trucks, where we were standing so tightly pressed together that they had difficulty in shutting the heavy doors, before bolting them. When the train did eventually move, it was unbearably hot, and there was no water or any facilities. The stench was gruesome. Some people fainted; others died standing upright.

It was just by luck, by pure chance, that we were not driven to the extermination camp Treblinka. Instead, we were taken to that pit of hell called Majdanek.

When the train eventually stopped and the doors were opened, the dead bodies rolled out. Roma and I couldn't pick up my father; we had to leave him behind. Outside we found some water dripping from a broken tap. Everybody was trying to get a few drops. And then I saw a familiar figure walking towards us in long white underwear. I realized it was my father. It was only after the war that I found out how this happened. Two young boys who were with us since the ghetto were ordered by the Germans to clean out the cattle truck. When they recognized my father, they pulled him out, and he came to in the fresh air. But not for long …

We were ordered to stand in a column, five abreast, and Germans with dogs on leashes paced on either side of us. I don't know what happened, but I tripped and fell as we were walking. As I was crawling to try and keep up with the others, a dog was biting into my back, and I was waiting to be shot. But the Germans thought this was amusing, and the dog was not called off of me until they had stopped laughing.

When we arrived at the actual camp Majdanek, which was enclosed by barbed wire, we were surrounded by sentries who pointed their rifles at us. Immediately, older women, children and mothers with babies were separated from us and sent to the gas chambers. And then it was the turn of the older men. And my father was among them. When he turned back to have a last look at Roma and I, he was hit on the head and bent under the blow. And that was when I saw my father for the last time. I have never, never seen my father again.

We young girls had to go through a *Selektion*. I whispered to Roma that I was afraid that I wouldn't pass the selection because of my bleeding back from the dog bites and the scraped knees from crawling on the gravel. Roma assured me she would follow me wherever I was sent.

With one wave of the whip—*rechts, links*— a human life was decided upon. Right, to life; left, to death. When it was my turn, I mustered all the strength I had left and lifted my shoulders and head high, and I was sent to the right: to life. And so was Roma.

After the showers, we were given lice-infested clothes and sent to a barracks which was completely empty. There wasn't even a piece of straw. We slept on the bare floor. There were roll calls twice a day. The watery soup with floating, rotten leaves was inedible. The morsel of black bread was gooey like clay, and the ersatz coffee was hard to swallow. Some girls couldn't take it; their bodies swelled up. Others got sick with typhus. They were all sent to the gas chamber.

I worked in different *Kommandos*, building roads and working in the fields. One such group was *Scheissekommando*. Our job was to push a wooden cart filled with faeces. Two girls were harnessed to the cart instead of horses, and the rest of us pushed from the back and sides. After the rains, when the wheels got stuck in the mud, we were beaten hard until we finally managed to get it unstuck. When we got to the field we had to release the cork at the back of the cart. We were then all covered in human waste.

One day, when we came back from work, we were all assembled in a big, open field. We had to watch one of our friends be sent to the gallows. When the SS woman kicked the box from under her feet, her body went limp. The commandant with shiny boots and white gloves and holding a whip in his white gloved hands announced: 'This is going to happen to any of you who try to escape. So that you won't forget it, you will stand here the whole night until the morning roll call.' We stood there the whole night, holding each other to keep warm, watching the little body turning in the wind while Roma spoke of the Shabbat food at home. She described it so vividly that we could taste and smell the different dishes.

One day Roma and I were sent to the men's camp in Majdanek along with some other girls. We were placed in an empty barracks. And when the men heard there were women in their camp, they rushed in: 'Have you perhaps seen my wife, Mary, she had long blonde hair?' 'Or my little girl, Stephanie, she had big blue eyes?' But they were chased out by the guards. The last man told us we were near the gas chambers. We then realized why we were brought there: we were going to be gassed. It was the middle of the night, and we were chased out by Germans with their barking dogs on leashes.

We were forced into a bathhouse which in reality was a gas chamber. When the heavy iron doors shut behind us, we stood there pressed together. We were crying, begging for help, and praying 'SHAMA ISRAEL', knowing that the poisonous gas would come out at any moment. I held Roma's hand and whispered: 'Don't be afraid; it won't hurt. I don't think it will even take long. We will soon join our loved ones.' And another miracle happened. Suddenly the doors opened. An SS man walked in, shouting *Ruhe!* 'Quiet! You are not going to be gassed.'

An order had been received to gas 500 Jewish women at this time, not 700, as we were. We were told that the correct transport of the 500 who were to be gassed would be arriving at Majdanek in the morning, and that we would be sent to another camp. When we were chased out at dawn, there was a contingent of women coming off the cattle trucks, and they were led straight to the gas chamber which we had just left. *Ordnung muss sein.* ('There must be order.') Due to German orderliness and the irony of fate, we evaded the Angel of Death.

We arrived in Auschwitz in cattle trucks. Only a few years ago I found out that they didn't want to accept us in Auschwitz. They wanted to send us back to Majdanek, as we were sick and some even dead. But the order was overruled, and we remained in Auschwitz. During our arrival there was an orchestra playing, made up of prisoners. In front of them were all the *Kommandants* of the camp. Among them was Dr Josef Mengele, known as the 'Angel of Death'. Then our arms were tattooed. My number was 48 632. Below the number was a triangle; this was the symbol for a Jew. Then all our hair was shaved off. I was calling for Roma. She was right next to me, but I didn't recognize her. After the showers we were given lice-infested clothes and sent to a barracks where we slept ten to a stone bunk, with only one blanket. At night, the rats came out from between the bricks and crawled over us. We got used to it. They were only looking for food. Sometimes the morsel of bread I kept under my head for Roma was eaten by them.

We stood at roll calls in the rain and in blazing sun, in the snow and freezing cold. We were then counted, and counted over and over until the SS woman came and received the report: so many sick, so many dead, and so many ready for work. I worked on building roads, pushing heavy trolleys, carrying heavy stones, heavy bags of sand and cement. When I think of it now, I don't know how I managed to do this very heavy work. But I knew I wanted to survive, and therefore I had to carry on. After the rains, my wooden clogs got stuck in the mud, and in winter the snow accumulated under the clogs; it was like walking on stilts.

Roma contracted typhus and was sent to the hospital. After the third day she was warned by the woman doctor—also a prisoner—to get out because Mengele was coming, and then he always ordered all patients to be sent to the gas chamber. Roma couldn't walk yet, but she crawled out and survived. But when I got sick with typhus, I was afraid to be sent to the hospital in case there wouldn't be anyone to warn me if and when Mengele was coming. So I hid behind the barracks and in the toilets, as I was unable to go to work. When the crisis was over and my temperature dropped, I joined the *Kommandos* at work. Then I had enteritis, and the toilets were far away. Those who were unlucky and did not reach the toilets in time would be punished severely. Our toilets consisted of a long stone slab with black holes on both sides.

During the winter, when the water froze in the taps, I washed myself with snow.

One day Roma begged me go to the electric fence with her. 'Let us end this struggle. In any case, the only way to survive Auschwitz is through the chimneys. So come, let us join our loved ones.' But the will to survive had been awakened in me. I wasn't yet ready to die. I convinced her that we had to carry on so that if we managed to survive, we would be able to tell the world what these murderers had done to us. At night, when the new transports were arriving from different countries in Europe, we heard foreign languages being spoken. In the morning it was all quiet. But the chimneys were billowing smoke and fire, and the smell of the burning of human flesh and fat was all over the camp.

There was a Belgian girl, Mala, in the camp. She was an interpreter and liked by all of us because she was so kind and good to us. She managed to escape with a Polish man. They were wearing German uniforms. Unfortunately, they were both caught and brought back to be hanged. Before she cut her wrists we heard her say to the *Kommandant* that the end of the war was coming and that they would have to pay for their murderous deeds.

When the new transports from Hungary began to arrive in 1944, I was selected for the position of *Blockälteste*, senior barracks inmate, as I was one of the prisoners who had survived the longest. This was a cushy job, but I refused, as it involved using fists and the whip and also reporting every occurrence of illness to the Germans. This meant that the sick were sent to the gas chamber. I didn't want blood on my hands, nor to be an instrument for the Germans or collaborate with them.

Once we were chased out of the block in the middle of the night. We feared that we were going to be taken to the gas chamber. But we were taken to the showers for a delousing. We were ecstatic that we remained alive, and we made a big commotion. Unfortunately, I was among the five girls who were to be punished by having their hair shorn to the skin for making so much noise. Our hair had already started growing back a little, making us look a little better. But with our emaciated bodies and with shorn heads, the five of us would certainly be sent to the gas chambers.

The nurse who was going to cut our hair was actually Jewish but was in Auschwitz as a non-Jewish Polish prisoner. She was known to me, as her sister was my friend before the war. I never let on to anyone in Auschwitz that I knew her. As she was about to shave my hair, I made eye contact with her. Without saying a word, I acknowledged with my eyes that I knew her, wordlessly begging her to help me. Mercifully, she pushed me back into the line without shaving my hair. Thus she saved my life.

While marching to work, the men's column was passing us. Moshe Baker, who had been hiding with us in the underground bunkers in the ghetto with his wife and child, threw a piece of paper to us, asking if we knew anything about his family. When his column was passing us over the following days, he threw one cigarette, and then a whole packet and more. We were 'rich' as we could exchange the cigarettes for bread, a piece of garlic or a potato.

In November 1944 I was sent on a transport: we travelled for two days and three nights in cattle trucks to Bergen-Belsen. Here there was no need for gas chambers or crematoriums, because people were falling like flies. They were dying of starvation and infectious diseases like typhus, TB and scabies. The corpses were piled up outside each block, and even inside. Having survived the uprising in the Warsaw ghetto, Majdanek and Auschwitz, I could not end up on the top of a stack of corpses in Bergen-Belsen now. The will to survive rose up in me with full force once again. I knew that I *had* to survive. And so it was: on 15 April 1945 we were liberated by the British army.

Words cannot express my feeling of freedom, but the most important thing was that we were alive, and that we could start living like human beings again.

In August 1945 I travelled from Bergen-Belsen to Warsaw with an older woman who protected me from the Russian soldiers. I had no money and no passport. My identification was the number tattooed on my arm and a fingerprint on a document I had received in Hanover. I went to Warsaw in search of my family, although I knew that they had all perished in Treblinka.

Yet I still had a spark of hope. One of my brothers managed to leave the Warsaw ghetto with his wife and daughter, and they went to live in a village near Lublin. I had always hoped that my little niece had been saved by the Polish peasants with whom they lived. And from Warsaw I made my way to this village, but at one of the stations I was warned by some Jews that I shouldn't travel any further, as there was a pogrom there and the Poles were killing Jews. I had to return to Warsaw. Later I found out that the three of them—my brother, his wife and their daughter—were among the Jews that were shot in the forest. There was an office where survivors left their names and where they could be reached. I put down my address as Bergen-Belsen. As I found nobody in Warsaw, I returned to Bergen-Belsen.

Through some British soldiers, we managed to contact Roma's father, who was my brother-in-law. He survived by getting out of the Warsaw ghetto and made his way through different countries before landing in Tel Aviv. He managed to get a visa for his wife and his four children, who were still in the Warsaw ghetto, to join him in Tel Aviv. Unfortunately, when the visa arrived in the ghetto, Roma was the only survivor. Her mother and her three siblings had already been deported. When he got the news that Roma and I were alive and in Bergen-Belsen, he used his influence to send us to Paris, where we were well looked after. Having received the visa, Roma left me in Paris to join her father in Tel Aviv. Almost two years later I joined them in Tel Aviv.

Six months later I met my future husband, a South African who was visiting Tel Aviv. Only thirteen days after we met, we were married. I became a South African by marriage and lived happily with my loving family in Johannesburg and Brakpan.

As I am one of the last generation of eye witnesses, I am now, in the twilight of my days, pouring out the terrors of my life in the Warsaw ghetto and in the three death camps, where disease, malnutrition and random killings were the constants of my life. They worked us to death on starvation rations. We were the slave labour brigade. These scenes will remain forever imprinted in my memory. I will never be able to erase them.

I still often ask myself why *I* was chosen to survive. Twenty-three souls of my immediate family perished. My parents, my brothers, my sisters, their spouses and eight nieces and nephews, including an infant born in the underground bunker in the Warsaw ghetto. I will never find an answer to this question.

So now, by spreading tolerance, learning and understanding, we survivors will be contributing to ensuring that these horrors do not happen again.

Maria Segal

Born on 15 June 1935. Deported to the Warsaw ghetto in 1940. Escaped from the ghetto in 1943; in hiding in various places in Poland until the Russian liberation in 1945. Lives in Santa Barbara, California.

I was born into a Polish Jewish family of seven children, the second youngest of five girls and two boys. My family and I lived in Okuniew, a small farming community about ten miles from Warsaw.

Okuniew was similar to many small European towns. It was centered around a small plaza, a square with streets branching out in different directions. The Catholic church was prominently located on one side of the plaza. The Jewish house of prayer, the synagogue, was on the other side of town. On Sundays I remember seeing Christian worshippers in their finest clothes.

We Jews observed our Sabbath on Saturday. I remember men dressed in dark clothes, some with black hats covering their heads. They were bearded and had side-burns. The older and more Orthodox women shaved their heads and wore wigs known as *shaitels*. My mother was too modern to shave her head. She had beautiful black, curly hair, as had one of my sisters and I. Our synagogue was an Orthodox congregation where men and women were not allowed to sit together while praying.

My father, Lieb Polonowicz, and his family were from Okuniew. My mother was from Warsaw. She didn't fit into life in Okuniew. My father was a very pious man. I do not recall him ever missing a Saturday morning service. My mother was not raised in an Orthodox home and was not as religious as he was. Still, she observed the Sabbath and the holidays.

In a strictly Orthodox home, cooking is not permitted on Saturdays; therefore, all meals had to be prepared by Friday before sundown. My mother would do the cooking and baking on Friday morning and afternoon. Since we didn't have our own oven at home, all the baking had to be done at the village bakery. I would help Mother carry the cakes and pastries to the Jewish bakery, to be baked in their large ovens.

The main meal on the Sabbath was taken at a large dining room table adorned by a traditional white damask tablecloth. The traditional Sabbath bread, called *challah*, was always served preceding the meal. My father would make a blessing, a *moitza*, over this special bread and break off small pieces of it to be passed around to each family member seated at the table.

As a young child, I was very happy to be part of a large family. I started school at a young age. The first language I grew up with was Yiddish. When I started school, I had to speak Polish. Apparently, I was a fast learner. I remember my first parent-teacher conference. My teacher told my mother that I had a *yiddishe kopf*, a Jewish head.

Okuniew was a small village, and we all knew each other, especially the Jewish people, as everybody went to the same synagogue. My father was a shoemaker. My brothers worked with my father. It was a trade passed down from generation to generation. His shop was at the front of the house, facing the plaza.

My family lived in the back of the shop. It was all on one floor. We got water from the village pump. In the backyard we had trees. I loved climbing trees. I would climb to the top of the cherry tree—I loved to eat the cherries. My mother was terrified and yelled at me to come down. I had a great deal of energy as a child and felt very alive. I was a carefree bird enjoying being outdoors and my freedom to run around.

I was five years old when Germany invaded Poland in 1939. There was a lot of uncertainty—much talk and speculation regarding what would happen when the Germans took over the running of the country. Everybody was worried about the scarcity of food. Since we lived in a farming community, we could generally count on a supply of potatoes, bread, milk and meat, and because my father was a shoemaker, he was able to repair shoes in exchange for food.

Shortly after the invasion the Germans began to put restrictions on Jews.

First, I was not allowed to attend public schools. Second, in order to further single us out, we had to wear white armbands printed with a large yellow Star of David. I had to put the armband on before I went out of the house.

The Germans did not permit the Jewish children to study at all. Consequently, we had to meet secretly in *cheders*, parochial schools. I remember meeting at the teacher's house, the Rebbe of Okuniew. This dedicated teacher risked his life when he took it upon himself to perpetuate Judaism through his teachings and to provide the village children with continuing education.

As soon as the Germans entered Okuniew they took away my father's youngest brother, our uncle Moishe. This frightened my grandfather so much that he died from a heart attack. Grandfather was a *shames* who took care of the synagogue. He was buried in the local Jewish cemetery next to the Catholic church and cemetery. I was very upset since I loved my grandpa deeply. Grandpa and Grandma lived a few doors away from us, and I used to go to their house often. My uncle Moishe and his family and children also lived nearby. All of them were taken to the Warsaw ghetto. I never saw them again. I don't know if they died in the ghetto or on the way to it.

Everything seemed scary and secretive in those days. German soldiers were parading around in their green uniforms and helmets, with carbines hanging over their shoulders. They always had fierce dogs. They never smiled much but always looked angry and unapproachable.

One evening there was a lot of commotion in town. The adults were rushing around, talking to neighbors and looking worried. Of course we children became agitated and wanted to ask questions, but we were afraid to because of the tension in the air. Finally, one evening my parents gathered all the children around the pot-bellied stove and broke the news to us about the unrest. Rumor had it that the Germans were planning to round up all the Jews in town and deport them to the Warsaw ghetto. 'It is possible that it may happen very soon,' I remember hearing someone say. 'Maybe as soon as tomorrow morning.'

My parents were very upset and worried as they tried to prepare us for the possibility of being separated. My older brothers and sisters were put in charge of looking after my younger sister and me. My mother and one of my older sisters sewed little satchels for the few belongings we could take. They made nametags with strings to hang around our necks. In each satchel we placed a few of our precious belongings, along with bits and pieces of food that we had in the house.

Our parents instructed us to stay together if possible. They told us that if we were taken to the Warsaw ghetto, we should meet at our uncle's house.

My mother had two brothers living in Warsaw and was sure we could live with them. We all had a very restless night, interrupted in the early hours of the morning by rasping German voices shouting through loudspeakers for all Jews to leave their homes and congregate at the town plaza. What a terrible sight: young and old with their worldly possessions on their backs, clinging to each other and trying to obey the German commands.

From then on it got worse by the minute. The soldiers had their snarling German shepherd dogs helping them divide the frightened townspeople into groups. The first bad and sad thing that happened to me was that I was separated from my mother and father. My father had to go to the side with the men, as did my oldest brother, Moshe. My mother was made to go on a different wagon—they had small wooden wagons hitched to horses. I was in a wagon with one of my older sisters, Shandulka. We didn't know where the rest of the family was. I was frightened, and my sister was extremely upset.

It took a whole day to get to Warsaw. When we finally reached the Warsaw ghetto, the Germans immediately ordered us to take off our clothes. They herded us into communal showers—men, women and children. I was very scared; I didn't understand what was going on. Then a fortunate thing happened: my whole family found each other in the showers. I was thrilled to be with my mother, father, sisters and brothers.

In the ghetto we were more fortunate than other families, as we went straight to Nowolipki Street where my uncle Itzak lived in a small apartment with two grown children. My uncle gave us one small room where all nine of us stayed. There was only one bed. My parents slept in the bed, and the rest of us took the floor.

Jews were not permitted to leave the ghetto. In some places there were openings in the wall, heavily guarded by the Gestapo on the Polish side and by the Jewish militia on the inside. Gentiles were permitted to enter the ghetto for business purposes. Many Gentiles took advantage of the situation by exchanging food for furs and jewels if cash was unavailable. Very often people would give anything they had for a piece of bread. The only goal at this point was survival, and it was most certainly the survival of the fittest.

My family had to find ways of sustaining ourselves. Our relatives were struggling to support their own household and were in no position to feed nine additional mouths. Food was scarce and extremely dear, and employment difficult to find. Almost every member of my family had to seek employment to be able to buy food. My father and two older brothers were fortunate to be able to work for a shoemaker. I can't recall what they earned, I just heard the family talk about how little money they were able to bring home. My three sisters found some kind of work in the clothing business. Even I, a child of six, worked by holding yarn for a lady—my two hands stretched out in front of me—so she could make it into a ball.

Sometimes I would go to the market with my mother and sister. It was an outdoor market, and my mother would complain about how expensive even potatoes were. She tried her best to obtain food to sustain the family with the limited resources we had. Most of the time Mother fed us soup—usually very watery. Bread was a true luxury, and we all lined up in the kitchen to get a piece. My mother rationed it very carefully, as there was usually not enough to go round more than once. There were many times, however, when we didn't have enough for even one piece per person. Since carrots were relatively inexpensive by comparison, my mother bought more carrots than anything else, and we would crunch away on them like rabbits. To this day I hate carrots with a passion. They bring back memories of the Warsaw ghetto and an endlessly empty stomach.

Although our whole family of nine occupied one small room, we were more fortunate than others who entered the ghetto without relatives already living there. At least we had a roof over our heads and a little food to sustain ourselves. Many people didn't have enough food and had no place to live. Many roamed the streets, searching the garbage cans for a few morsels of food to be consumed.

Some of the people walking the streets were so emaciated that they resembled human skeletons clad in rags. I was shocked to see these persons who were hardly able to walk and who collapsed on the street. Even though I was a child, it made me pause to think about the value of life and the vulnerability and helplessness of human beings.

Many of these people not only starved to death, but were unable to get a decent burial when they died. Once their bodies collapsed, they were covered with newspapers lying on the street. After a time their skeletons were loaded onto wheelbarrows and carted off, most likely to the nearest dump. No one really cared or worried about what happened to anyone else: we were all too concerned with our own survival.

Because of the bodies lying in the street, the stench was at times very pungent and disease common. Typhus reached epidemic proportions. Medical help was almost nonexistent and besides, no one could afford to pay a doctor. We hoped and prayed not to get sick.

Then, in 1941, we started to notice that the ghetto was shrinking—the Germans decided to make it smaller and subsequently eliminated several streets. We also noticed that they began to deport Jews from the ghetto. The Germans deported Jews from the ghetto every day. They generally did not tell people where they were taking them—if they did, the typical explanation was that they were taking them to labor camps. Only later did we learn that each day the Germans rounded up hundreds of men, women and children, loaded them onto trains and took them to concentration camps in Poland: Auschwitz, Treblinka, Majdanek and others.

When no one returned from these deportations, we began to sense that something was wrong: the Jews taken on the trains were not coming back. Eventually the remaining Jews in the ghetto formed a group of resistance fighters. Although they did not have access to weapons, they used all possible means to arm themselves. This handful of Jews, under the able leadership of Mordecai Anielewicz, fought back in April 1943. The struggle lasted 28 days—until the Jews were defeated.

Fortunately, or unfortunately—I am not sure which was better—I did not remain in the ghetto to the bitter end of the fighting and the subsequent liquidations of Jews. A Gentile woman from Okuniew named Stasia entered the ghetto about once a week. Stasia was a businesswoman who knew that the Jews in the ghetto were desperate for food, and she would bring food in exchange for money or valuables.

On one of her visits to the ghetto Stasia asked my mother if I could go back with her to Okuniew to look after her cow. It was decided that I would leave the ghetto with Stasia since I could help my family in this way. Some of my father's customers owed him money for shoe repairs and shoes he had made for them prior to deportation. When I came back to Okuniew with Stasia, I went out to the surrounding villages and collected what he was owed. Thus I was able to amass some food and money to bring to my family. I did this twice. My family was overjoyed when I returned to the ghetto with bread, potatoes and even some chickens. We had a true feast.

The third time I left it was impossible to get back into the ghetto. Security at the walls had become extremely tight, and the guards would not let us in. Stasia and I tried multiple crossings, hoping that some other guards would be more lenient. But we had no luck with either of them and turned back toward Okuniew.

That was the last time I saw my family. I felt very sad that no one from my family escaped the ghetto—except me, alone. I was seven years old.

I will never forget my mother's expression the day I left with Stasia for the first time. My mother was standing by the kitchen window, with my little sister looking on. After a few minutes she said to me, 'Go. You are the only one in the family that has a chance of surviving, because all of us will be killed sooner or later.' That really bothered me, because my true intention was not to be the only one to survive. My hope was to go back and forth between the ghetto and Okuniew and help our family to obtain food. After

I lost contact with my family, I could not stop thinking about my mother's last words to me.

In Okuniew I went to live with Stasia and her husband, Janek. It was difficult. I had recurring dreams about various members of my family, especially my mother. One afternoon, as I sat outdoors reflecting on everything that had happened to me, I became a little drowsy and fell asleep. When I awoke, I was very frightened. In my dream I saw my mother, and when I tried to talk to her, she did not respond. She looked like a piece of marble, and I could not communicate to her how much I missed her and how much I needed her to be part of my life. It was very difficult for me to accept my separation from my family. I refused to accept that my family might perish any time and that I might never be able to see them again.

Not long after I left the Warsaw ghetto I was outside watching the sunset. In the distance I could see red flames jutting out from burning houses in the ghetto. I felt helpless and sad. My family might be in trouble, and I could not help them. From Okuniew I watched the ghetto burn.

Stasia and Janek were heavy drinkers. They loved their schnapps and made their own vodka from potatoes. When they had too much to drink, they often argued. At times they screamed at each other so loudly that I would get scared and run across the road to Stasia's parents' house. The Polanskys, like most of the people in Okuniew, were farmers. One day when I came to their house frightened, they asked me to stay and not go back to Stasia's house. I was very happy to get away from that chaotic household.

As time went on, I became more used to the family. But I never ceased thinking about my parents, brothers and sisters. One evening after dark there was a knock on the door. What a welcome surprise—a familiar face from the past: Toba and her boyfriend. I knew Toba from before the war; she and her family owned a grocery store in Okuniew. Like the other Jews in the village, Toba and her family were deported to the Warsaw ghetto at the same time as my family. When the destruction of the Warsaw ghetto began in April 1943, Toba and her boyfriend managed to escape before they would have been taken to a concentration camp. Both made their way back to Okuniew.

Toba had some news for me. She told me that before she left the ghetto, she saw her family and my family being taken from the apartment by the Germans, most likely to concentration camps in Majdanek or elsewhere. That was the current rumor as to where the Jews were being deported. Toba stayed for a short period of time. We embraced, and she left, cautiously, in fear of being recognized by someone in the village. Before she left, Toba gave me a snapshot of my sisters and brothers—a picture I still treasure. I have few photographs of my family.

Two days later I was told that the Germans had picked up Toba and her boyfriend, taken them to the local cemetery, and shot them. Unfortunately, someone squealed on them, and they had to die so young just for being Jewish. I wondered if I would be the next victim. Although most of the Poles in the village knew my whereabouts and did nothing to harm me, I was still very scared.

A few days after the death of Toba and her boyfriend, as I sat in the kitchen with the Polanskys, there was a knock on the front door. Mrs. Polansky went to the door and asked who it was. When the voice replied 'Police and Gestapo', Mr. Polansky immediately pushed me out the back window and into a cornfield and told them that I no longer lived there. After the police had left, the Polanskys came out to the cornfield to give me food and a blanket. Together we decided that it was no longer safe to remain in their home. Apparently, the Germans had decided to round up all the remaining Jews in town, and I was on their list.

The cornfield became my living quarters for several days. I walked from there to the nearby woods, remaining in hiding at all times. Mr. Polansky was very kind. He always found me and brought me food to eat. At night he came again to check on me. I could deal with the days much better, wandering around here and there in the fields or woods. When night fell, I got frightened of the dark, and any slight noise scared me. I felt lonely when thinking about my family. I continuously had bad dreams of running and being chased.

While living in Okuniew after leaving the ghetto, I had made the acquaintance of a young Gentile woman and her family. Wanda was in her twenties with very pretty dark long hair and a beautiful face. Wanda got married to Jurek, who lived in Warsaw.

After the wedding, Wanda moved to Warsaw. When I was no longer safe in the Polansky household, Wanda sent word through her mother, telling me to come to Warsaw to live with her. I then started to plan my escape from Okuniew. I thanked the Polanskys for taking care of me. They risked their own life to protect me.

Thus, in the spring of 1944 I fled back to the city I had escaped from one year earlier. Early one morning, while everyone was asleep, I packed a few of my belongings and started walking toward the train station, which was about three miles from the Polansky home. When I arrived in Warsaw, Wanda was waiting for me at the station. We went directly to her grocery store in the town center. Now that I was in the big city I had a sense of safety. No one knew that I was Jewish, and my 'Aryan' features helped me conceal my Jewish identity. Wanda had a spacious apartment, and I helped out in the store. No one suspected I was Jewish, and when people asked, Wanda told them that I was her daughter.

The tension between the Germans and the Poles in Warsaw mounted. Bombings and air raids increased every day. One morning, as Wanda and I got ready to leave for the store, the sirens began to screech, and we had to go down to the basement shelter. It was not the first time this happened, but this time it was different. After several hours of hiding we were suddenly interrupted by two uniformed German soldiers ordering us to come upstairs. The Germans then loaded us on their trucks and took us to a large open field. At the field they took all the men, old and young, while all the women and children remained. As we waited, we heard gunshots in the near distance.

We tried to maintain our composure, but it was difficult. There was a lot of crying when the soldiers lined us up, their rifles pointed in our direction—the direction of the women and children. One of the older German soldiers tried to console us. He told us that he, too, had a wife and children at home and did not enjoy his assignment. He was merely carrying out orders.

The suspense of the unknown was painful, and each minute seemed more like an hour. At the precise point when the guns were getting ready to fire, a miracle occurred. A tall, uniformed German officer on a white horse appeared out of nowhere and charged in front of the firing squad. This god-like human being raised his right hand, shouting *Halt!* Slowly, the firing squad dropped their weapons and retreated gradually, one by one. An enormous sigh of relief emanated from the frightened group of women and children. Our group was then escorted to a nearby church for the night. Although the church was cold and we had to spend the night on the hard benches, we were grateful to have another chance to be alive. The question now was: what next?

Early in the morning the following day, our group was escorted by the German soldiers to Płaszów, a temporary camp, to process us for transport to a concentration camp. First, we had to submit to a medical examination conducted by a team of Polish doctors. They took it upon themselves to paint us with yellow chalk and tell the Germans that we had jaundice. Since the Germans were terrified of contagious diseases, they took the doctors' advice to let us go.

At the time of departure from Płaszów I was on one side, and Wanda was on the other side of the lines. I ran across to Wanda to make sure that we were not separated. We had no home, no money, and did not know where to go. Wanda remembered that her husband had paid for a summer vacation on a farm in the country. 'Let's find the farm,' she said, 'and see if they would be willing to let us stay there while we look for Jurek.' Jurek was in the Polish resistance, and we had no idea whether he was dead or alive. Wanda's younger brother was also in the resistance, and prior to our leaving Warsaw she had learnt that he died in the Warsaw insurrection.

We found the farm and were allowed to stay there for a while. One evening, as Wanda was reading the newspaper, she came across a list of wounded soldiers, Polish and German. To her great surprise she saw her husband's name. Jurek was convalescing in a hospital in Kraków, recovering from injuries sustained during the fighting between the Poles and the Germans. The next day we went to Kraków to see him.

Wanda found a small apartment for us in Kraków. We had no means of support. But Wanda was an entrepreneur—she started a small business selling bread on the black market. I was always by her side, helping out whenever I could. As soon as Jurek was ready to leave the hospital, he joined us in the apartment and got a part-time job teaching.

The war was still on, and we heard that the Russians were getting closer to Kraków. One evening in January 1945 we heard a bulletin that said that the Germans had left Kraków. The next morning the Russians marched into the town. We put on our coats and went over to the town square in the town center. People were yelling and screaming happily as we watched the Russian troops approach the Polish Citadel. This was one of the happiest days of my life since I had been separated from my parents, my sisters and brothers.

The end of the war gave me a new hope that perhaps I could find some of my family. When the excitement of greeting the Russian soldiers was over, I began to write letters to the International Red Cross in Geneva. People were scattered everywhere, so many were looking for lost relatives. Special areas were set up to locate each other. I seized the opportunity to try to find my family, if any of them were still alive.

After several months I got a reply from the Swiss Red Cross. They had located a cousin of mine who went to Russia before the war broke out in 1939, and he was now back in Poland. But when I wrote to my cousin, I just got a reply stating that he had moved on without leaving a forwarding address. This was a big letdown to my hopes that some relatives might still be alive.

In the meantime Wanda and Jurek found a small apartment in Bydgoszcz. Wanda enrolled me in school. I was now 11 years old, and she put me in a fifth grade class although I had not attended school for all the war years. The first day at school was miserable—I knew nothing, and the other kids laughed at me. But I worked hard, and the following year I did so well that the teacher selected me to represent the school on a two-month vacation in Denmark. That was a wonderful experience. I stayed with a family named Larsen; they lived on a small farm on Fyn island.

Following my return to Bydgoszcz I started the eighth grade at school. All this time, I never gave up hope and continued to search for my real family. I had some recollection of an uncle named Abraham living in Paris. He was a younger brother of my father, and when I was a little girl in Okuniew he used to visit us with his wife. Before going to Denmark I had written to my uncle, and to my amazement I heard back from him. He wrote that he wanted me to come to Paris to live with him. Although the unknown was scary, I decided to accept my uncle's invitation. It was sad to leave Wanda and Jurek, who had been my family for the past five years. They had saved my life.

After many complications I arrived in Paris. I stayed with my uncle Abraham and his family, and after some time I got enrolled in a Polish boarding school. I loved it and learnt a lot. I got friendly with my Latin teacher, Mrs Spanow, and she introduced me to a Jewish couple from Montreal, Canada. They wanted to adopt a young orphan without any family attachments. I had made up my mind that I was too old to be adopted. The idea of going to Canada, however, was appealing, and the Spanows helped me to make contact with the Canadian Joint Committee, which sponsored young Jewish children and helped them emigrate to Canada.

I crossed the Atlantic on the Cunard Line in July 1950. Coming to Canada meant starting a new life, and I had to learn a new language. At first I stayed with families in Quebec City and Montreal. I learnt English quickly and did well at school. Later I attended McDonald College for two years and obtained a certificate to teach up to the eighth grade.

I married in 1958. My husband, David, was from New York City, and after my graduation from Sir William University we bought a house in New Jersey, where we settled and started a family. We had three children, and it was a sheer delight to see them grow up together.

In 2003 I arrived in Santa Barbara, California, and became involved with the Jewish Federation of Greater Santa Barbara, where my story is featured in a permanent exhibit, 'Portraits of Survival: Life Journeys during the Holocaust and Beyond.' I am now a volunteer for the Portraits exhibit and speak to many groups of all ages about my experience, growing up in Poland and as a first-hand witness of the Holocaust.

It took me 50 years to talk about my experiences. I did not talk about the Holocaust to my children or my husband. Now I find that sharing my experience helps me to deal with the past. It is important to inform young people about how destructive and damaging anti-Semitism and prejudice of any kind can be. It is imperative that we teach the new generation to be kind and accepting of people of different religions and races.

The reason why I speak is because I have seen what hate can do. Hitler hated the Jews, and many of those who supported him did so too. It is important to forgive. But the fact that my family is gone … I have a hard time forgiving that.

In 1996 I traveled to Poland with the Jewish Heritage Travel Group. I asked the tour guide if I could hire her to take me to Okuniew for a visit. I was nervous and had mixed feelings about going back to my village where no one in my family was alive. But I was hopeful to find some familiar faces that could give me some information. Once again I was disappointed. We did not find anyone or anything from my childhood. The synagogue was gone; my home as well as the homes of my uncles and grandfather were destroyed. Our next venture was to find the cemetery where my grandfather was buried. This was heartbreaking for me: the Jewish cemetery was completely leveled and overgrown with weeds. On the other hand, the Catholic church and cemetery were intact and beautifully groomed.

At the end of my trip, I flew to Bydgoszcz from Warsaw to visit Wanda and her family. The reunion was very emotional. Because of Wanda I made a second visit to Poland in 2008. I had received a letter informing me that my rescuers—Wanda and her husband, Jurek—had been recognized as 'Righteous among the Nations' by the Israeli Embassy in Warsaw and Yad Vashem, the Holocaust Museum in Israel. I owe Wanda my life and would not miss the opportunity to witness this presentation for anything in the world. When I was asked to deliver a speech at the ceremony in Warsaw, I decided to do it in Polish since it was predominantly a Polish audience. I started off by saying that I am alive because Wanda saved my life. Handing Wanda the medal and diploma, the Israeli ambassador quoted: 'He or she who saves one life saves the whole world.'

I have been riddled with guilt for surviving. I miss my family terribly, even though they have been lost for almost 70 years. I cannot forget them—there are constant reminders. As I think about them and reflect on my memories, I can almost see my mother standing by the kitchen window, although I can hardly recall what she looks like. Too many years have passed for me to have a clear view of her sweet, gentle and loving face.

Judith Meisel

Born on 7 February 1929. Deported to the Kovno ghetto in 1941 and to the concentration camp Stutthof in June 1944. Escaped during the evacuation of prisoners from Stutthof in June 1944, under heavy bombardment. Arrived in Denmark in February 1945 and remained there until the end of the war. Lives in Minnesota, USA.

I was born in Lithuania, in a little town called Jasvene. My family consisted of my father and mother, my brother Abe, and my sister Rachel. We had cousins, aunts and uncles, second cousins—146 people living in Jasvene were somehow related to the Beker and the Friedman families. My father was a merchant dealing in lumber and cattle. My mother, Mina, was an incredible woman. She felt that girls are just as important as boys and gave us all an education—taught us at home. She was a most incredible woman.

My family life was deeply rooted in Judaism. The Jewish community would get together, especially on the Shabbat. My father would always bring a guest. There was always room for one more person. I think that the person I am today is due to my very early upbringing in Jasvene.

I will never forget the day the Rabbi and two men came to my mother. Afterwards she told us that our father had died. After my father died my mother moved with me and my brother and sister to Kovno [Kaunas] to find work. The big city fascinated me because we had come from a small *shtetl*—a small town with a large Jewish population. We found a place to live near the synagogue. The synagogue was all blue. The women sat upstairs, the men downstairs.

In 1940 the Russians invaded Lithuania. And things became chaotic. We weren't allowed to go to the synagogue any more. Mother could no longer light the candles openly. The school teacher asked us if there were any religious services held in our home. She did not mention Jews. But my mother said we would have to be careful.

A man came to our house and said, 'They are burning Jews in Poland.' Everybody said: 'He is crazy. He is senile. Why would the Germans, an educated people, burn Jews?' Nobody wanted to believe him.

When the Germans invaded Lithuania in the summer of 1941, women were holding flowers in their hands, welcoming them because they were happy to get rid of the Russians. My mother was very scared and began to hoard food. But we were trapped. Nazis came into the courtyard and shouted: *Achtung! Achtung!* 'We want you Jews to come out of the house.'

My mother was still in the house collecting our things. They pulled her out by her beautiful black hair and beat her up. As we were moved away, people spat on us and threw things at us. I kept asking my mother, 'Why do they hate us? What did we do to them?' And she answered, 'It is because we are Jews.'

This I couldn't understand, because we were friends with all the families, and I played with the children in the courtyard. Now they were throwing stones, and the parents were egging them on. When I think of the word 'anti-Semitism', that is exactly what that was.

I could hear *Schnell! Schnell!* ('Quickly! Quickly!') as we plodded across the bridge over the Neris River to the place which became the Kovno ghetto—the closely guarded, barbed-wire-enclosed area of small primitive houses and no running water. We lived with three other families under terrible conditions. But as my mother used to say: 'At least we are alive.' The food we got in the ghetto was very sparse. I got to the point where I would eat almost anything, even grass.

A Jewish man named Motke asked me if I would like to help feed my family and others in the ghetto by getting food from the black market. I said yes. He organized children who didn't look Jewish—who had blond hair and blue eyes like me—to sneak out of the ghetto and smuggle food back in at great risk. I remember that for a diamond ring I got five loaves of bread.

When the ghetto was established, the Germans selected a group of leaders from the Jewish community. They in turn selected a Jewish police force. Most of the policemen were fine, but there were some who were horrible. Arnstain was head of the Jewish police. He was a cruel man, and I feared him.

At the ghetto gate I had a loaf of bread under my arm. He said, 'Lift up your arm.' I said, 'It hurts.' He said, 'What do you mean, it hurts?' And he gave me a smack—and the bread fell out. He beat me up, and he said, 'If I catch you one more time, I'll kill you.' There were people who were so hungry that they stole; if discovered, they were immediately put to death. The Germans used us as slave labor. We had to work in a factory making shoes for the German army. At the end they put chains on me, which made the work harder.

One afternoon in June of 1944 we were ordered to assemble in a large field. We stood there waiting for a long time. It was raining and cold. Then we were taken into trucks—my sister, my brother, my mother and me. We drove for about two days. In the middle of the night we were transferred to a train and taken to Stutthof concentration camp in Poland.

When we arrived they separated the men from us. I remember my mother—she was devastated when they took my brother. And that was the last time I saw my brother in the camp. We went into Stutthof, and all I saw were these huge mountains of shoes. I asked my mother: 'Why are there so many shoes?' There were piles and piles. And she said, 'Why are you asking questions all the time?'

We had to get into one line. And they gave you a striped dress and clogs which we had to wear all the time. My mother had gold teeth. And they just yanked them out; my mother's face was full of blood. I had long blonde hair. I had the Gestapo lady on my left side, and the Gestapo guy on my right side. And they both had fun pulling my hair out. The male Nazi said to the SS woman: 'Such beautiful blonde locks; I will take it home to my daughter. She would love it for her doll.' When I got back to my poor mother, there was blood all over my head—and over her face.

One episode in Stutthof made a strong impression on me. Right in front of me was a young woman. Later I found out her name. It was Chavah. She wore a dress; she had to undress, and a little baby fell out, an infant. The Nazi guy picked up the infant, threw it against the asphalt, and killed it.

Chavah was assigned to our group. We were in a wooden barracks, three, four, or five to a bunk bed—I was in a three-tiered one. Chavah was next to me. She would not open her fist; she had something in her fist. I told her it was okay at the same time as we all asked: 'What do you have in your fist?' It was a tiny baby shoe. When the Nazis found out, they wanted to take it away. When she refused, they put a bullet in her head.

73

We stood to roll call every day without knowing where we would be taken. At this time my sister was not there; she was very ill with typhus and was in a hospital. My mother and I were standing together when they came to take my mother, not me. We didn't know where they would take her, and I said, 'I want to be with you.' So she took my hand, and together we went to the gas chamber. We had to undress, and then we were led into a room. There was a small step, and my mother was already inside. There was a guard drinking beer, and he shouted, *Schweinhund! Heraus!* I was holding my mother's hand as he was pushing me out the door, and my mother said, 'Run, run, Judi!' And that was the last time I saw my mother.

Then I was outside, naked, and there were some trees where all the bodies lay. Some women saw me and shouted, 'Come here!' I ran towards them, and they immediately surrounded me, put a dress on me and said, 'Run back to your barracks!' Which I did.

I don't remember what happened afterwards, I was in such shock. I went to see my sister and said to her, 'You have to come out. We don't have a mother now.'

Outside the gas chamber there were two large logs. They put bodies on the logs, poured gasoline over them, and there were these big pyres of burning bodies. I felt this constant smell—the stench of death. I thought, 'That is how I am going to die.' Among the dead I would close my eyes, and I would think of the smells I felt as a young girl in Jasvene. I would smell the flowers at home and the bread my mother baked on Friday morning. And most importantly, I would hear my mother's voice as she sang a lullaby to me. Thus, in my thoughts I went back to my happy childhood in Jasvene.

In December 1944 there was an announcement that Stutthof would be demolished and that everyone was to assemble by the gate to march out. It was bitterly cold, and the wind was howling. If you didn't walk fast enough or if you fell, you risked being shot—they were constantly shooting people. We kept walking all day. I kept saying to Rachel: 'Walk. Walk. We want to live. We want to live.' And all of a sudden the sky opened up with bombs, and everybody started to run, the guards too. My sister asked, 'What are we going to do?' We saw a light and a house and walked across the fields towards it. We only had clogs to walk with; my sister had two right clogs, and we stumbled and fell. At last we reached the house. There were two women and a man—a Russian, a prisoner of war, we found out later. One of the women almost seemed to know we were coming. She immediately brought us clean clothes, tore off our striped dresses, and threw them outside because they were infected with lice.

The woman gave us the clothes and something to eat, a kind of soup which I threw up because my stomach was so shrunken. She also gave me a scarf to cover my head. But she still told the Russian man to take us to the *Umschlagplatz*, a rounding-up place for Jews who were to be deported. Instead, the Russian told us to change our names and pretend we were Catholics, so that the Germans wouldn't suspect we were Jews. He also told us to walk to the Vistula river, which was covered with ice in the winter, and to crawl all night on all fours across to a convent on the other side. He believed we would get help there.

We both feared that we would be left alone, and also that we both would not survive. We both thought about it but didn't tell each other. From the moment I arrived in the ghetto in Lithuania, I didn't know what the next moment would bring. My sister and I didn't *plan* to survive. It was *mazel*, 'luck'. People say to me, 'You are a survivor. You are brave.' From the time in the ghetto in Kaunas to the time in Stutthof, everybody was brave; all wanted to live. Whether you did was just a matter of luck.

We finally reached the convent. We did not have to tell them: they knew we were Jewish. We thought we were the only two Jews alive, and we only wanted to survive as Jews. After they told us we had to convert in order to be safe at the convent, my sister said: 'We can't stay here. We're going.' And we left without them knowing.

When we left the convent, I was very sick with typhus. My sister said, 'I'm going to take you to the hospital in Danzig. And when they ask you who you are, you point at your mouth and say you are *stumm*—'mute'. And she left me on the steps of the hospital.

The method worked—I was taken into the hospital. In a couple of weeks my sister came with a lady whose name was Mrs Arnstain. She said that we were going work for the German army. Mrs Arnstain was in charge of a *Wehrmacht* station, a place where the Germans came to eat and stay overnight. Here we were, two Jews, disguised and working for the enemy! Mrs Arnstain had eleven children. She was the cruelest person. She would beat us at night, and if we did something she thought was wrong, she would beat us again.

One day the German soldiers came to get food, and one of them asked Mrs Arnstain: 'Who are these two girls? They look so emaciated.' And she responded, 'They are Lithuanians. Don't worry, they don't stay in the house. They stay in the barn.' And one of the soldiers said, 'Isn't that funny? We just come back from the Kovno ghetto. We just burnt it. There are no more Jews left.' And they started drinking and singing. My sister said, 'We have to be very careful. Maybe we should leave.'

And we started to make a plan for where we should go from there. But we couldn't, because the bombs were raining down on us. At one point the soldiers tried to force us into an air-raid shelter. My sister said, 'I'm not going. Please, God, let a bomb fall and kill me. I can't go on.' Just then a bomb fell on the air-raid shelter. We were jumping and hugging each other. 'Thank God, thank God! We're alive!'

One day Mrs Arnstain said that we were going to Denmark. We really didn't want to go. We didn't even know where Denmark was. It turned out that we had very little choice. For they told us they were going to let out the sewers and flood the whole area. We sailed from the harbor in Danzig. While we were sailing out of the harbor, the bombs were falling. As soon as we had reached the open sea, the boat was torpedoed. I don't know how long I was in the water—I don't remember. All I remember is being numb. I was hauled out of the water and into a small boat. And then we were taken to Denmark. At that point we were separated from Mrs Arnstain. This was in February 1945.

We arrived in Denmark, and we were immediately put into trucks. They took us to a big gymnasium in a town called Swinge. They gave us food, and we could walk anywhere we wanted to, provided we came back at dusk. There was a woman at the gymnasium. We asked her where the Jews were. She said, 'When you Germans' (she thought we were Germans) 'are in concentration camps, the Jews will return.'

They asked everyone who was not German to step forward. I said to my sister, 'I'm afraid to tell them we are Jewish. What if it is a hoax? They will find out we are Jews, and they will kill us.' But she said, 'No. We have to do that. The war is over.' So we went over to the Red Cross lady and said we were Jewish. The woman stood up, almost crying, and asked us to prove it. So we signed our names in Hebrew. She gave us a big hug, and she said, 'Do you know where you are?' And we said, 'We know we are not in Germany.'

When they weighed me, I was 47 pounds, and I was sixteen years old. They gave me a flowered kerchief, and I never took off that scarf; I wore it all the time.

Rachel still thought that we were the only Jews in Denmark. We were curious—were there any other Jews? Then a woman said, 'In a couple of weeks the Jews will come back.' And I remember my sister asking, 'How do you know there are Jews left?' And she said, 'We know. We helped them across to Sweden.' In 1943, while my sister and I went through the Kovno ghetto and Stutthof concentration camp, the Danes saved their Jews by taking them across to Sweden.

I feel I owe my life to the Danes. Not only my life to live, but they also gave me back my self-esteem as a human being and a sense of trust. I saw that not all human beings are as bad as the Nazis were, or as those who collaborated with the Nazis. Here is a people—I couldn't even talk to them!—and look what they are doing for me, how nurturing and how caring they are.

We experienced the liberation of Denmark in Swinge and were then brought by truck to Copenhagen on May 5, 1945, to Endrup school. I will never forget the day. Two people came up to the school. They were standing near the gate. A woman told us in German that they were Danes and that they would like to take us out and show us Copenhagen. To us, this was heaven.

Their names were Paula and Sven Jensen. They were Lutherans. They had no children, and they created an incredible family for us along with other Danes. They were so kind to us. Paula took my kerchief off, and when she saw all the wounds, she started crying. When she took me to the doctors, they didn't think my hair would grow back. But she vowed she would see to it that my hair grew back. One of the doctors said she could put egg yolks in my hair and then put me out on the veranda to sit in the sun with my kerchief off. I was getting sicker and sicker. I had TB, and my stomach had shrunk so much that it was difficult to digest food—you name it, I had it. Paula took me to hospital. They admitted me and nursed me back to health. And Paula did it—I got my hair back.

Paula came and picked me up with a wheelchair and took me and Rachel to the harbor to see the largest group of Jews coming back from Sweden. My sister and I couldn't believe it. These were Jews! Other Jews had survived! We were not the only ones!

I will always have that deep feeling of loss because most members of my family were murdered by the Nazis. And yet, there at the harbor I was exhilarated—people were smiling, people were hugging each other, people were crying, carrying flowers, stretching their hands out to welcome the Jews back. And the king, Christian X, was there. So was the chief rabbi, who made a special blessing. To me, that was the rebirth of me and my Judaism. We have a Jewish saying: 'May the Jewish people live.' The Danes helped the Jews live.

I thought that if Jews have survived here, then perhaps some members of my family had survived too. I will never forget a day in September 1946. I was still in Denmark, and we got a postcard from my brother. He was alive! It was unbelievable. We thought he had died, but he survived Dachau. He was writing from Italy at the time, but he later moved to Toronto.

My sister married a Dane and had a child. I wanted to leave Europe. No matter how wonderful Denmark was, I wanted to go to Toronto and live with my brother.

When I told Paula I was leaving, she could not understand. She was just crying and holding me and saying I couldn't go. *Min lille pige*—'my baby'—she called me 'my baby' all the time. And it's true that she nursed me back to life. She had a motto that when you say 'thank you', you should say 'Thank you for everything'—not just for one thing, but everything. And that is what it says on Paula's tombstone: *Tak for alt*—'Thank you for everything.'

When I left Copenhagen, she came running after the train, crying: *Min lille pige*—'My little girl, don't leave me!'

Aboard ship, I met my first husband, and in July 1949 I came to Canada, to my brother. I had no idea what my brother looked like, and at first we didn't recognize each other. I got married in 1950, in Toronto, and then we moved to Philadelphia. And I have three wonderful children.

I went back to school. I worked very hard to obtain my degree in early childhood education from Temple University in Pennsylvania. I wanted to do this because I was never really allowed to be a child, to be a teenager, to have an education. My childhood was so disrupted that I feel I have never really had one. I feel most comfortable when I sit with the children on the floor, with little children on my lap, reading a story to them. And I love to cook with them—to measure and weigh and taste. It gives me satisfaction, because those are the things I longed for during my imprisonment.

One night in 1963 I was listening to the news. An African-American family named Baker had moved into an all-white neighborhood in Folcroft, Pennsylvania. A lot of white people turned out, screaming and yelling at them and throwing all kinds of debris. And I was devastated, because here we were in Philadelphia, in a city of brotherly love—and it was like the *Kristallnacht* in 1938, the 'Night of Broken Glass' when the world sat and looked on what was happening in Germany, but did nothing. So I made some cookies, and I went to the Bakers to wish them welcome. I was called 'white trash' as I was walking by the whites standing outside the Bakers' house. But I felt that if their homes were not safe, my home was not safe. And if their rights as blacks were trampled on, my rights as a Jew were trampled on at the same time.

I was a Holocaust survivor. But I could not talk about it. I did not want to traumatize my children. But that incident with the Bakers made an incredible mark on me. I knew that I had to tell my story. At that point I became involved in the Civil Rights Movement. And as a 'Panel of American Women', made up of a Catholic woman, a Protestant woman, an African-American woman and myself, we would speak everywhere we were invited, all over the country.

I will never forget the March on Washington. I was very lucky: I met the Reverend Martin Luther King twice, and it was just exhilarating to hear his great speech, 'I have a dream', in August 1963. I think those were the most exciting times.

Racism. Bigotry. It is still happening all over the world. And we have to constantly fight against it, to try and ensure that it does not happen here—or anywhere. We cannot afford to say, 'What can I do? I am only one person.' One person can do a lot. Who is responsible? The world is responsible for letting something like that happen.

If none of us had survived the Holocaust, none of us would have been able to tell our story. To tell about the Holocaust from a historian's point of view is quite different from telling about it from an eyewitness's point of view. These are two different things, and I am thinking about this a lot.

I always wanted to go back to Lithuania, to retrace my steps. Something there was just pulling me to go back. And eventually, in 1992, I did go back with my husband.

In 1941 the Nazi *Einsatzgruppen* went through the villages in Lithuania. When they got to Jasvene, they rounded up all the Jewish people living there, marched them out of the village, and ordered them to dig their own grave. All the 146 members of my extended family were massacred and are buried in that mass grave. Among them were 43 children. You cannot measure suffering.

They wiped out generations and generations to come. Never in my life would I have dreamed that *I* would have children, or that I would become a grandparent. Aaron is my oldest grandchild. When I held him for the first time, I thought of all the children who did not survive, who were my age, and who would now have had grandchildren. I was holding him for all these people—and especially for the people that were with me in Stutthof. We who were there all promised each other that we would remember—to tell the story of what happened to us.

I can remember without going back to Lithuania, or Stutthof, or Denmark. But there is something about standing on the ground—being there. In Hebrew we have a proverb: *nekama*. It does not mean 'revenge', but just standing there and saying: 'I am alive, in spite of all.'

I cannot forgive the Nazis, but I have nothing against Germans. The twentieth century was the most brutal in human history. For me, the Holocaust stands by itself. How could it happen in a highly cultured nation like Germany? I agonize about it every day.

We cannot allow ourselves to forget what happened. If we forget, we do so at our own peril. As a Holocaust survivor, I cannot stop talking about my experience. We don't know what will happen when the last witnesses are gone. The world is getting smaller and smaller, and yet we know less and less about each other. We must respect each other's differences.

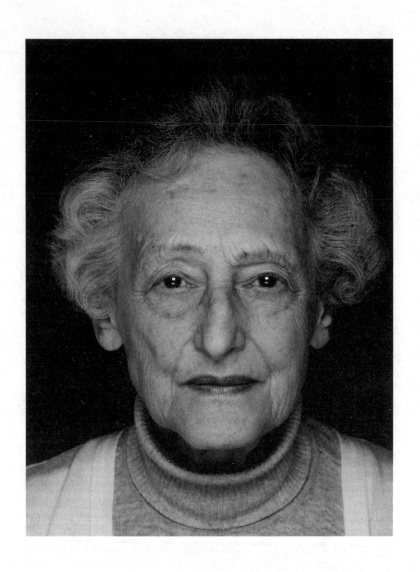

Isabella Wolf

Born on 22 January 1932. Deported to Szolnok in June 1944 and from there, via Strasshof, to Heiligenkreuz in Austria. Walked in spring 1945 from Austria to Budapest and from there took the train back to her home town. Lives in Oslo.

In 1922 my father, Imre Weisz, opened a timber yard in Körösladany with his brother-in-law. Körösladany is in south-east Hungary, not far from the Romanian border. There were two children in my family: my sister Eva and I.

When I was very young, I had a good childhood. I had friends and went to school like other children. I was the little sister in the family, as Eva was five years older. She learned how to play the piano when she was very young, something we all enjoyed.

In 1944 I was twelve years old. At that time Eva was living in Budapest, where she was receiving instruction in sewing and singing techniques. On 19 March German troops occupied Budapest. The same day they arrested Jews in a raid near the train station. Among those who were arrested was Eva, who was trying to catch a train back home. We received a phone call from Budapest saying that Eva had been arrested by the Germans. Mother answered the phone, and fainted.

Only much later did we find out what had happened to Eva. She was first sent to an internment camp in Hungary, Kistarsca, and after six weeks there, on to Auschwitz. She arrived at Auschwitz on 2 May, 17 years old. She did not return.

The German occupation was the start of our nightmare. Up until that point I had not noticed that anti-Semitism was becoming more invasive. Yet there was quite a lot that inconvenienced us Jews. It became more difficult for Father to run his business when the so-called 'Jewish laws' were introduced in the late 1930s. These laws restricted Jewish enterprises. They also prevented me from starting grammar school. There could not be more than three Jews in each class, and they should preferably be boys. I did not start grammar school until after the war, when I returned from deportation.

People often bullied us at school. And when we were going to the synagogue wearing our nice clothes, youths would come up to us and torment us. They called us 'fucking Jews' and threw horse dung they picked up from the street at us. So I often arrived at the synagogue with black stains on my clothes. All the same we were, for the time being, able to continue to live fairly quietly and peacefully—disregarding these bullies.

Following the invasion on 19 March our situation radically worsened. Shortly afterwards German troops arrived in Körösladany as well. In April our house was confiscated. It was going to be used as a hospital for an SS battalion that was going to the Eastern Front. We were allowed to keep one room in the house where we could stay for the time being. This was the situation at Easter 1944. *JUDE* was painted on Jewish houses. We had to wear a yellow star, which we had to sew onto our clothes. Not long afterwards we were ordered to move into a ghetto which consisted of our synagogue, a school building and a cantor's flat. We were given a space in the school building along with my two aunts and their families. My maternal grandfather was also there with us.

We were in this ghetto for a few weeks before we were deported. We were taken to the neighbouring town in horse carts. The Hungarian Gendarmerie—a sort of police force—guarded us. We were told to bring food and clothes—as much as we could carry. At the railway station in the neighbouring town there were cattle trucks which we were loaded into. So were Jews who had been collected from other places nearby, so there were many trucks that were filled with people.

The train drove to another town. Fortunately, it was not very far, perhaps 100 kilometres. When we arrived, everybody had to get out of the cattle trucks immediately. The elderly who were not that agile were kicked by the guards. In this town, Szolnok, there was a former sugar factory. That became a rounding-up camp for Jews in the county. Almost 5,000 Jews were packed in together here. On arrival we were met by both Hungarian police and SS men. They hit us, young and old, to make us move faster.

There was no room inside the factory, so we had to sleep outside. We were only there for about a week, but it rained a lot. We had baked bread and cakes which we had brought with us in bags. These bags became the 'beds' we slept on. We heard crying and screams from people who were beaten and abused. Several people became so filled with despair that they took their own lives.

In particular, Jews who were well off were interrogated about money and jewellery the Nazis believed they had hidden away. We also met relatives from other parts of the county. In the desperate situation we were in, it was not a pleasant reunion.

We were a big family with aunts, uncles and grandparents. My uncle, who was Father's business partner, was given the task of dividing the group from our little town in two. Without having any idea of the consequences, he wanted our family to be gathered together in one of the groups so that we could help each other.

We were the lucky ones. Our group was sent to Austria, the other to Auschwitz. The Jews from the other small towns were also divided in this way—so that one half was sent to Auschwitz and the other half to Austria. We were many young and old people in our group, as many of the men under fifty had already been sent to labour camps. Of the fifty who were deported to Auschwitz, only a few survived.

The stay in Szolnok was a nightmare. It was a terrible experience to be completely at the mercy of people who obviously wished us harm. When we crossed the Austrian border, the first stop was the transit camp Strasshof. We were thoroughly inspected. We women were also subjected to a pelvic exam, as someone might have hidden something there. We experienced this as highly offensive. We still carried our bags filled with bread, now mouldy.

After a week we were sent to different places to work in agriculture or in factories. There were also a few who were transported to Vienna. We were sent to a place called Heiligenkreuz—an estate with a monastery, churches, private houses, and labourers' cottages. We were perhaps fifteen from our family who were sent there. There were eight to ten of us to a room. I slept in the same bed as my mother. The elderly could be placed on kitchen duty They made food for us, and they also looked after the children.

It turned out that Heiligenkreuz was a camp where you could survive. We were ordered to work in the fields, and in the forest in the winter. I worked alongside the adults. I was not particularly strong, but this way I got more food. In the winter we sorted potatoes in the cellar, which was an opportunity to steal a little to supplement our rations.

I remember particularly well one episode which could have been very dangerous for me. I was standing on top of a threshing machine, working, and dropped my pitchfork into the machine so that it stopped. There was a frightful fuss, because at first the guards thought it was sabotage. It would have been straight to Bergen-Belsen. But when the estate steward found out that it was a child who was up there—a thin twelve-year-old girl—the guards were reprimanded, and no further investigations were made. The steward was a friendly man, a fairly nice Austrian. I do not think he was a Nazi.

There were many nationalities and prisoners of war on the farm. There was a Ukrainian who flirted with one of the Jewish girls of around 14-15 years. The girl's father objected to this—he wanted to protect his daughter. For that reason, the father was sent to Bergen-Belsen, and we later found out that he did not survive. Such episodes meant that you could disappear. We had no say; in reality we had no rights.

Even though we did not actually starve, the food was bad, and we got rashes and big, ugly sores from vitamin deficiency. We were infested with lice and vermin, and there was a lot of quarrelling due to the way the food was allocated. Every day during the last months of the war we could see large groups of planes heading for Vienna to bomb the city. We hoped the war would soon be over.

Some of the labourers told us what they heard on the BBC about how the front lines were changing. The Russians were approaching from the east and were pushing the German soldiers into retreating. This created a dangerous situation for us. Among the German soldiers were SS soldiers who were tasked with liquidating any Jews they came across. It is unbelievable, and chilling, that this was a priority task for the SS even though they were under severe pressure from the Russians.

An Austrian overseer saved us. When the situation became dire, he led us into the forest by the estate. I think the steward knew about the plan to lead us into the forest, to survive there during the critical phase.

This overseer held his hand over us, and it was he who let us know when it was safe to come out of the forest. I think both he and the others who helped us were part of the resistance, but I do not know. In any case they sympathised with us. They said we could come out of the forest, as the Russians had occupied Heiligenkreuz.

We spent the night in a school. Then we were going to try to get back home to Körösaladny. There were usually many horses by the school, but now they had all been confiscated and stolen. We found a cart on which we placed the children and the elderly, and then we had to pull it ourselves.

The war was not yet over, and while we were walking eastwards, we came close to the front. The soldiers were shooting at each other all around us. It soon became apparent that we had to be extremely careful around the Russians. As we were pulling the cart along the road, one of the women suddenly disappeared. A little while later she managed to run back to us, and she told us that she had been raped by Russian soldiers. Little by little we heard about more rapes, and that made us less happy to see the Russian troops. The way we looked, we may not have been terribly tempting, but the danger of rape was looming.

I cannot remember how long it took us to walk from Austria to Budapest, but it took several days. Each night we had to find somewhere we could shelter because we did not dare be outside at night. It is strange that we managed to walk all that way under such difficult conditions.

In Budapest the Germans had blown up all the bridges [between Buda and Pest], but makeshift pontoon bridges had been erected across the Danube. I think we, like everyone else, tried to register at a Jewish centre. From Budapest we took a train heading east to where we lived. The Russian troops also used the trains as transportation, and on our train people were even standing between the carriages. Still, the most important thing was getting home to Körösladany as soon as possible.

This was in late April or early May, just before the war ended. My father and a few other men had already returned in late 1944. They had been doing forced labour in a part of Hungary that was liberated by the Russians as early as October-November 1944. They had also hidden in a forest, as there were many who were killed by retreating Germans. After he had returned home, Father tried to get hold of some of our possessions that had been stolen or confiscated.

Mum and I returned home alone. We got separated from the others when the Russians tried to take us prisoner by Wiener Neustadt on our way to Budapest. It turned out that the Russians wanted labourers, and we became so frightened that everyone ran in separate directions. Mother and I could not find our way back to the others, so we walked on, just the two of us. We were not the only ones on the road—there were people from many different countries. I remember an episode when a truck stopped next to us. Pulling the cart had made us tired, and we wanted to climb on board, but then we discovered that the truck was full of prisoners from another camp. The prisoners were ill, probably with typhus. Mother said that we could not ride along here, and we continued on foot.

We arrived home exhausted and teeming with lice, but alive. My father and my little dog welcomed us ecstatically. When we were to be deported, all the Jews' dogs were sent to a man who was to put them down. But this man knew Father, and he spared my dog. And when my dog saw me, he recognised me immediately and was delirious with joy.

The lice-infested clothes were thrown into the fireplace, and gradually we began to recover. The others arrived home a little later—and those who had been in other places in Austria and in Theresienstadt, even later still.

After the war Father started up his business again, and I went to grammar school in Szeghalom. But in 1950 we moved to Budapest because Father's business in Körösladany was taken from him and he was in danger of being arrested. After the communists had risen to power in 1947, private businesses were gradually nationalised. Often those who were a little well off were arrested immediately. Father realised what could happen, so he saved money so that he could buy a flat in Budapest. We were not completely safe there either, but at least we were safer than in Körösladany.

Then there was the uprising in the autumn of 1956, and our situation became very precarious. I was in favour of change because I had seen what communism could lead to. At the same time there were signs of anti-Semitism among those who supported the uprising, so the situation for us Jews was complicated. The uprising was a protest against the communist government and its close ties to the Soviet Union. The revolt spread to the rest of Hungary, and the regime was toppled. But the Soviet Union invaded Hungary on 4 November, and many civilians were killed.

And so people began to flee across the border. That had become possible because the land mines on the Austria-Hungary border had been removed in the spring of 1956. Along with some relatives, I fled too. I had so many bad experiences in Hungary that I thought I had to try somewhere else. Then I came to Vienna. Most of all I wanted to go far away, preferably all the way to Australia. It was not possible to get entry permits to Australia, but, along with my relatives, I was given the opportunity to come to Norway. We arrived in Kristiansand in December 1956 and stayed there for two years. I moved to Oslo in 1958 after my parents had arrived in Norway the year before. It was a difficult time. After a while I got a job at the Norwegian Radium Hospital. A doctor we knew from Hungary got us a flat. We were grateful for that, as it was difficult to find housing.

My husband originally came from Transylvania, which is in southeast Hungary, bordering Romania. After the war he lived in Israel for twelve years. He wanted to be a pianist and studied at the Tel Aviv Conservatory of Music. In September 1956, shortly before the Soviet Union invaded Hungary, he participated in a Liszt competition in Budapest. The following year he was in a Smetana competition in Prague. We started to exchange letters via an acquaintance, and he moved to Norway in 1959. We married at the City Hall on New Year's Eve 1959, and a little later in the synagogue.

I worked at what was then called Norsk Hydro's Institute for Cancer Research. There I worked on tissue enhancement and with testing various medications. I was 'Senior Lab Technician'. I had a university degree, having studied Biology and Chemistry in Budapest from 1950 to 1955.

I worked at the Institute for Cancer Research for ten years. Following that I stayed at home with the children for a few years. I am lucky enough to have two sons, and I am happy that they both live in Oslo. They are a good support for me, not least now that my husband has passed away after several years' illness.

In 1975 I started at the central laboratory at the College of Veterinary Medicine. I was a bio-engineer there for 22 years. Afterwards I have been a pensioner here in Oslo. I am a member of the Jewish congregation and have tried to be of service in various matters. When my husband became ill, I saw it as my life's mission to take care of him.

It is important that the new generation is informed about the Holocaust. It was incomprehensible to us that our children did not learn anything about the Holocaust in school. In that context, starting the White Buses in the 1990s was a particularly important initiative. Many time witnesses have been on trips arranged by the White Buses and *Aktive Fredsreiser*, and they have told Norwegian youths about their experiences. Blanche [Major] is among those who have put a tremendous effort into this. I have been on a trip with the White Buses to Auschwitz, along with Blanche. I was impressed with how thoroughly the teachers had prepared the students and with the good work they did.

It was strange, and difficult, to come to the camp where my sister Eva was murdered by the Nazis. And it was special to be there with the youngsters and their teachers. After all, the young people did not have the same connection to Auschwitz that Blanche and I have, but they were visibly affected by what they saw. It was terribly sad to be in Auschwitz. But at the same time it was encouraging to see that the work that we missed when our own children were at school was now being done.

Having the Norwegian Center for Studies of the Holocaust and Religious Minorities and Oslo Jewish Museum is valuable. Time witnesses like Samuel Steinmann do a great job—he is the only one left of the Norwegian Jews who were sent to Auschwitz. So there is a lot of information work that is being carried out by fantastic people, thank goodness. That means there is hope the Holocaust will not be forgotten, and that knowledge about this terrible crime can be carried forward to the next generation.

Edith Notowicz

Born on 16 March 1929. Deported to Auschwitz in May 1944, then on to Hainichen in October 1944 and finally, in April 1945, to Theresienstadt, where she remained until the end of the war. Lives in Trondheim.

I come from a small rural community in southern Hungary, near the Romanian border. We were a family of five. Dad owned a sawmill; he made sleepers, parquet flooring and other building materials. Mum had studied music in Vienna. She played the piano and took an interest in social work. There was a *Waisenhaus* (home for orphan children) in the nearest town, and Mum was involved in that. She used to give small concerts to raise money for people in need.

Aunts and uncles and several cousins lived close by us. Mum and Dad thought it was important that we kids had respect for both humans and animals, and they taught us from an early age that all humans are equally valuable. At the same time they gave us the freedom to make our own decisions. We were close, and we had a good life. We were not spoiled and got on well with each other. The highlight of the day was when the whole family was gathered around the table to eat. My brother was fourteen years older than me, my sister twelve years older. So I was the youngest, the afterthought.

Hungary was put in a difficult situation when the war broke out and both Austria and Czechoslovakia became parts of Nazi Germany. The Nazi ideas spread in Hungary as well, and anti-Semitism was on the rise. In addition, more and more people believed that Hitler was invincible and that the only thing that would save Hungary would therefore be to establish closer ties with Germany.

This alliance with Nazi Germany became Hungary's undoing. For even though Hungary contributed to the German war effort, not least by sending soldiers to the Eastern Front, that was still not enough for Hitler. In early March 1944 he sharply criticised our Regent, Miklós Horthy, and on Sunday 19 March, German soldiers marched into Hungary. Horthy and his government were sidelined, and so the Nazis had free rein.

This was the start signal for the extermination of us Jews. The way we noticed the changes was through all Jewish children being thrown out of school. We were no longer allowed to travel. Rationing was imposed on both food and clothes and shoes, without us being given ration cards. At first those of us who lived in the country had an advantage, as we could grow our own food. But many people were hostile towards us. Soon the order was given for all Jews to wear the yellow Star of David. This decree applied to all Jews above the age of six.

On the morning of 5 May there was a knock on the door at home. When Dad opened the door, there were policemen outside. They said we were going on a transport and gave us an hour to pack some essentials.

This was a shock. Admittedly, we had heard rumours that Jews were being arrested and sent to Germany. But we knew little about what happened to them because none of them returned to tell us about it. Dad found out about the arrests, but it was too late to get away. Mum found out as well, from her little brother. But his wife was a Nazi, and she said: 'Don't you dare escape, or I will report you.' So we were taken, the whole family.

What to bring? Mum was in a difficult situation. She tried to pack some clothes and a little food. We had no idea if we would ever return to our house. At first we were sent into a forest. We stayed there for a fortnight while we were waiting for onward transport, without knowing where to. Fortunately, we had summer temperatures, so we managed tolerably well even though we had to sleep in the open air.

Then one day we were told that we were going to be sent on, and we were transported to the nearest railway station.

I remember the train ride well. We were put in carriages without windows, only a slit near the top. There were about 60 of us in one carriage. Without a toilet or anything. There was only a bucket in a corner, but that filled up quickly, and the contents spilled out across the floor. The smell made people nauseous, and they threw up. Mum and Dad tried to comfort my sister and me as best they could. But since they knew so little, the adults could not manage to hide their worry either. People died in the carriage. We sat on the dead.

We were not given water or food; we got nothing. I cannot remember how long the journey lasted, but it was several days. There were bombardments too, and then the train had to stop. The carriage doors were locked, so it was impossible to escape.

Finally, the train slowed down. The brakes screeched, and the train jolted to a stop. The next moment the doors were flung open, and I cannot forget the sight that met us. On the platform there were many soldiers, several of them with German Shepherd dogs. They yelled that we should get out of the carriages. When they thought we were not fast enough, they pushed us and swung their rifles around, hitting us. It was chaos beyond compare. It was not easy for us to move quickly; we had a strenuous train ride behind us, and most of us were in bad shape.

We had arrived at Auschwitz. In the midst of the chaos I heard the famous tune, 'La Paloma'. The alluring rhythms did not at all fit in with the hell we had entered. The music may perhaps have been a deliberate attempt at defusing the arrival; I do not know. For me, the whole thing turned into a horrid experience. In all the confusion I was separated from my parents and my sister. The soldiers were yelling, but I could not understand what they were saying. I saw the soldiers gathering women and children on the one side and men on the other, but I could not find my family.

And so I was shoved into a group of other children. It was a terrible experience. The security of my family was suddenly gone. I was surrounded by snarling dogs and bellowing soldiers while the columns of men and women disappeared in different directions. That was the last day I was with Mum, Dad and my sister. I do not know whether they went straight to the gas chamber or whether they were used as slave labourers for a while; I do not know. That parting was final.

'La Paloma' is a lovely tune, but for me it evokes dismal memories. Memories of extermination.

A few more children were also left behind, and together with them I was taken to another part of the camp. Here we were put in a separate barracks. We had to take off our own clothes, and then we were 'disinfected' and shorn of our hair. It's an incredible change that takes place when one moment you have long black hair and the next your head is totally bare. The same thing happened to the other children. Both male and female guards ordered us around. Like the other children, I tried to ask if anybody had seen Mum and Dad, but nobody knew anything.

We got hardly any food the first day. We had to sleep in stalls—on planks without mattresses and without blankets to cover us. We were 10-12 children in each stall. We were terrified of what was going to happen to us, and we did not have any adults to talk to. The other children had been on the same transport from Hungary as I had, so we spoke the same language. Fortunately, I ended up in the same stall as a girl who was three years older than me, Ilona Weisz. We soon became good friends. She looked after me, and we tried to stick together.

All the time I was dreaming about Mum and Dad returning so that we could go home to our house in Hungary. Mum would prepare good food, and we would be together forever and everything would be nice. That was just a dream. Mum and Dad did not come to collect me, and gradually I had to come to terms with the situation. Even so, I and the friend I shared a bunk with would lie there and talk about what we were going to do when we got out of the camp. We had many plans, especially horse riding. These chats were good therapy for us. We had something to look forward to, and it helped keep our spirits up. We thought we would soon get away from this gruesome place, but we were wrong.

The notorious Doctor Josef Mengele, also known as the 'Angel of Death', operated in Auschwitz. I soon made his acquaintance. Mengele used children in his medical experiments. He had a special predilection for twins, but I can't go into details here. It is too horrible for me. He was also interested in finding new methods of sterilisation and thereby preventing the Jewish race from procreating. In the camp he had more than enough test subjects, and I was one of those who were used in Mengele's sterilisation experiments on Jewish girls. There was no question of sedation. The pain is still with me, and in the dead of night it sometimes is as if I am back in the experimentation room in the camp.

Everything was taken away from us. Absolutely everything. I often find myself thinking: Is it true or not? What was the driving force behind the Nazis' intense attempt to exterminate other people? Is it possible that humans can be like this? Often I cannot believe it. But I have been there, so I know it happened.

A head count was carried out every morning and every evening. We had to line up outside the barracks. Those who were in charge often took a long time to count us—while we stood there, shivering and freezing. I do not know if somebody was missing, or if they just pretended that the count had fallen short. In any case, they started over again several times.

The odour of the camp has also stuck in my memory. The crematorium ovens were continuously in operation, and the smoke and the smell from the chimneys spread out like a blanket over the camp when the wind came from one particular direction. It was awful. Even though we children at the time did not understand that what we were smelling was burned human flesh, we associated the crematorium with something painful and frightening. I realised that there was something grim going on over by the crematorium. There were so many people who walked in that direction—large processions, but we never saw them again. When somebody told me what was going on there, I refused to believe it. In my world there could not be humans who were that mean, but it was true, of course!

The reason I was not exterminated as well was that the Nazis needed labour. I was set to work in a factory a short distance from the camp itself. We had to march out of the camp each morning and having worked twelve hours in the factory, we marched back again. We had to carry planks and rocks and do hard physical work. Fortunately, it was warm when we first came to the camp, but in autumn the cold arrived. We had poor clothes and were cold.

I was strong because I had played a lot of sport. Mum taught me to play tennis. Dad taught me to ride and swim. This helped me cope with the work. But our food rations were small, and little by little, I was drained. We saw those who could not take any more and who threw themselves at the electric fence. That made a powerful impression on us children, for the guards let the dead remain hanging on the fence to put fear into us. One day I fell asleep from exhaustion while I was at work. One of the guards discovered this and immediately fell on me. I was wide awake within the span of a few seconds, and I got a thrashing like I had never before had in my life. That a grown-up person can beat up a defenceless child in that way is completely unfathomable.

In October I was sent from Auschwitz to a town called Hainichen. I was on a transport with several hundred Jewish women who were considered to be fit for work. In Hainichen there was a factory that made military equipment, *FRAMO-Werke*, where we were going to work. We were billeted in a camp with a fence and watchtowers around it.

We had to work twelve-hour shifts in the FRAMO works. It was hard work, and we were not given enough food. Twice a day we got a thin soup, and in the evening a little bread. It was a cold winter, and we had thin clothes and were cold a lot.

One day in the middle of April 1945 we were told that we were going to be evacuated from the camp. The Russians were marching on Hainichen, and they could be there any moment. I cannot remember the route we took, but one particular experience has stuck with me. We were near a factory complex. Suddenly, we heard a loud hum, and we were told to stop immediately. The next moment the planes came like an angry swarm of bees and started dropping bombs over the factory site. The German guards disappeared to try to get to safety while we prisoners were left standing there.

It is strange, but the bombing raid did not make me scared. I ran around with Ilona and counted how many bombs had fallen. Close by the factory there was a river, and some of the bombs exploded in that. As a consequence, dead fish floated to the surface. This was food—and the bombs exploding nearby could not be helped. Ilona and I waded into the freezing water and picked up all the fish we could get hold of. We were so hungry that we ate the fish raw, and the skin and bones as well.

Our evacuation route ended up in another camp, Theresienstadt in Czechoslovakia. When we arrived, it was very chaotic—a number of prisoner transports had arrived from the east. Some of the prisoners were ill with typhus, and thus contagion was a fact. The sanitary conditions were terrible.

Fortunately, I was placed in the same barracks as Ilona here as well, and we continued planning our future. This night we talked about how we would enjoy delicious food now that the war surely was soon at an end. We told each other how we would prepare the food and serve it to all our friends. We continued to daydream in this vein until we fell asleep.

When I woke up the next morning and spoke to my friend, I did not get a reply. I tried to shake her a little so she would wake up. To my horror, I discovered that she was cold and stiff. I had seen so many dead people within the past couple of months that I immediately realised that she was dead. She had quietly taken her last breath in the night—as if someone had blown out a candle. It was a great sorrow to me when she was carried out of the barracks, put on a cart, and taken away. I do not know what they did with her. Most likely she was taken to the crematorium and turned into ashes.

Now I had lost the person who was closest to me. And even though I was only a child, I began to prepare myself for soon going the same way as my friend. Where we were was still a forecourt to hell. Here we lay, hungry and frozen, and there was shit and dirt everywhere. Around me prisoners died in droves. At the same time we heard the roars of canons not far from the camp.

The camp command realised that it was only a matter of time before the Russians would be there, and they tried to escape. The first Russian forces took Theresienstadt on 8 May. The war was over. Imagine if my friend had lived just a few more days—I think she would have survived as well.

The Russians immediately began a rescue operation to save as many of the prisoners as possible. But they were in a desperate race against time.

Many of the prisoners were so weak that they could not handle the strain, and succumbed.

Even though the war was over and the camp liberated, several weeks went by before we could be sent on. That happened at the beginning of June. That was when the first prisoners were released. The German soldiers and guards who had not managed to escape were arrested as soon as the Russians took the camp. The roles were reversed. Earlier we were the ones who had had the hair on our heads removed; now the Germans had a broad stripe shaved on their heads. We had been ordered by the Nazis to wear the yellow Star of David; now the Red Army made sure that those same Nazis had a swastika painted on the front and back of their jackets. Then they were made to do forced labour in the camp, heavily guarded by Russian soldiers.

I first ended up in a children's home and was there for a period while the Red Cross tried to find information about my parents and siblings. It was in vain. After a few months I realised that I was the only member of my family who had survived. So I was sent back to Hungary.

That was a shocking experience, as I soon realised that there was no place for me there. I was simply not welcome. New people—who, I did not know—had moved into my childhood home. They did not want to talk to me and downright chased me away. The new owners were communists and represented a red dictatorship. But the communists did not welcome the Jews either. What made it particularly problematic for us Jews, was that few countries wanted anything to do with us.

I lived for a while with a friend of my dad's. I helped him with various practical matters. I graduated from grammar school, and then I studied law for a while in Kolowzsvar. Later I worked for a barrister. We knew about the uprising in Budapest in 1956 and the brutal way in which it was subdued by the Soviet Union.

I met my husband in Israel, where I lived for seven years in the 1960s. I worked for Schindler, a Swiss elevator factory in Tel Aviv. Then I came to Norway in 1969 and have lived here in Trondheim since. For nearly thirty years I worked at The National Museum of Decorative Arts and Design (*Nordenfjeldske Kunstindustrimuseum*).

Even though it is now more than sixty years since the war ended, many of us still have scars. The nightmares came later, and the anxiety they caused me made my nerves fail. I was only a child when I experienced the worst terrors of war, and I believed that the anxiety would pass when I had become an adult. But the bad memories have haunted me since.

Even though I have experienced the Nazis and their atrocities, and even though I myself have been a prisoner at Auschwitz, I have difficulty believing that this could have happened in enlightened Europe. Sometimes I get the question, 'Why were you saved?' I cannot give an answer, for I do not know why specifically I was saved.

I have been back in Hungary to look for my childhood home. It does not exist any more. But the walnut tree Father gave me when I was ten, that is still there. I was so happy to see it!

I have been back in Auschwitz as well. The first time was in 2006, and I was there together with a school class that was on a themed trip with *Aktive Fredsreiser*. The memories grew incredibly powerful, and it was very difficult for me to walk around the camp. Not least when I saw the large pile of hair that was exhibited in one of the display cases. Suddenly, I was back in the barracks where they shaved my hair off. The huge mountain of suitcases was also a sight I struggled with. My thoughts went back to the day we were chased out of the carriages and had to leave our luggage on the platform. Perhaps some of what we brought with us is in some display case or other in the museum? It was a difficult trip, but that meeting with the interested Norwegian school pupils gives me hope.

It is disconcerting when one hears that somebody denies that the extermination of the Jews ever took place. It is particularly awful when these persons manage to trick young people into this web of lies. If a lie is repeated often enough, it can be thought to be true.

I have been imprisoned in Auschwitz myself, and I lost my childhood in Auschwitz. I personally experienced the Nazis' devilry and am one of those who survived this hell, against all odds. All of Europe failed the Jews. What is it going to be like the day the last of us goes? Will there be nothing to check those who deny the Holocaust?

When I returned to Hungary after the war, I did not have a single anchoring point in my life. With the starting point I had at the end of the war, things could have gone really badly. I could easily have ended up as a streetwalker or an alcoholic. Fortunately, that did not happen even though everything was utter chaos both inside me and around me. A human is stronger than an ox and weaker than a fly. You can handle more than you think, if you have to. I had to find my anchoring point myself—and I did. My anchors are nature and good people. Others have found different anchors in their lives. We must respect other political and religious viewpoints.

I have always wanted to be of help to other people, and I have involved myself in helping drug addicts here in Trondheim. I have my own motto: 'Help, don't disavow, what you see around you!' One might perhaps say it is my own political manifesto. In that I have but one article: 'You shall not hate, or regard the differences between humans, but regard what we have in common.' To me it does not hatter whether it is a Jew, Christian, Buddhist or Muslim. We ought to try to find a common platform and respect each other. I think it is only then we will be able to build a peaceful coexistence.

Yvonne Engelman

Born on 9 October 1931. Deported to the Berehovo ghetto in 1943, and from there to Auschwitz in the autumn of 1943. Sent on a death march to Peterswaldau in late 1944, and remained there until the end of the war. Lives in Sydney.

I come from Czechoslovakia, but not from a large town. I was born in a place called Dovhe, in a beautiful part of the country. I have wonderful memories of my childhood—until I was seven and half years old.

Ours was one of about 200 Jewish families in the village, which is located in the Carpathian mountains. We had no electricity, and only outdoor toilets. We were peasants, but there was also a sawmill. Life was hard and quite primitive compared to now. This part of the Carpathians has belonged to different nations. Before I was born, it was Austria-Hungary, then it became Czechoslovakia, and now it is part of the Ukraine. We went through great changes. I went to a Czech school, and I still speak Czech fluently. You never forget what you learn as a child.

I had a wonderful childhood. I was the only child, and I was spoilt—but spoilt with a lot of attention and love. I had many Jewish and non-Jewish friends, and I did not encounter anti-Semitism while I was growing up. Everybody respected each other; there was no hostility.

When the Germans and the Hungarians came, everything changed. We became ostracized, businesses were confiscated, and life became very difficult. This all happened because we were Jewish—we had done nothing to provoke the Germans. My father was taken to the police station at least twice a week. And we never knew whether he would return or not. I was very close to my dad. One day he came back and his front teeth had been knocked out. It was a very traumatic childhood after the war started.

In 1943 our family was sent to a ghetto which was in the town of Berehovo. The ghetto used to be a brick factory. All the Jews from the surrounding areas were brought here. The conditions were bad—both the hygiene and the food. We were in one big room, and we lived with great anxiety, not knowing what was going to happen the next day. The uncertainty was the worst thing. To this day I suffer from anxiety since I lived with anxiety for all those years.

When we had been in the ghetto a few months, the SS came. This was at the end of 1943, and there was no warning that they would come. They were doing selections. We were taken to the railway line. When we arrived at the railway, there were cattle trucks. We were marched into those trucks. They were so crammed that we could hardly stand. Then they locked the doors, and we were travelling. But nobody knew what our destination was or where we were going since we had no contact with the outside world. There was hardly air to breathe, and we were packed like sardines. In the morning the doors were opened. They removed the buckets where you were supposed to relieve yourself, and each of us was given a thin slice of dark bread and something to drink that looked like coffee.

On the third night my father said to me: 'Look, I'm not sure where we are going. But I'm sure we are not going for a holiday. I want you to promise me that you will survive.' I said, 'Of course I will survive.' I had no idea what he really meant by it. Because, you know, at the age of twelve and half ... and we were not sophisticated children. We were truly *children*; childhood was different then.

We travelled like that for five nights. On the fifth day, they opened the doors, and we had arrived at Auschwitz. I had no idea what that place was. But when we arrived, some of the girls from our township were already there. One of them asked, 'Why didn't you commit suicide before you came here?' She raised her hand and said, 'Can you see that smoke coming out of the chimney over there? That's where your parents are burning.' We all thought that she had lost her mind. She also said, 'I helped build the barracks where you will be staying.' We had no idea what she was talking about.

We were marched out of the trucks. You can imagine how we looked—without sleep, without water, without food. On the platform there were dozens and dozens of SS. One in particular caught my attention. Later I learned that his name was *Doktor* Mengele. He had a baton in his hand. He came to the row where I was standing with my parents and my grandmother. He took my mother away from me. They went to the left, and I went to the right. But none of us knew what that actually meant. My mother was 38 years old. They were young people. Today I have children who are older than my parents were.

That was the last time I saw my parents. Those of us who went to the right were marched into an enormous hall. And in that hall there were many SS. We had to undress, and then they shaved our hair off. To this day I do not know what happened, but I was actually marched into a gas chamber. The gas chamber was a room with showers, but instead of water there was gas. And they locked the door. We were in that room all night. But then in the morning we were marched out. The gas did not work.

So we were taken to a wash room. That was an enormous room with water taps. The water was bitterly cold. We had to wash ourselves. Then we were given a grey dress, but no underwear, and wooden clogs. That is what they handed out to us. Then we had to walk to the barracks.

The barracks were wooden huts with three-tier wooden bunks. When we got there, it was already night-time. We were five girls in each bunk. We had just one grey blanket. We had not been given any food. They switched off the light, and we had to go to bed. In the morning the SS came while it was still dark. They switched on the light and marched us out into the yard. We had to stand three girls in a row, with our hands on the shoulders of the girl in front of us. They let us stand there—one hour, two hours—regardless of whether it snowed or rained. They did not care. They were counting and recounting, and if you as much as blinked an eyelid, you were struck with a baton across your face and on your body. I don't hear well in one ear; my middle ear was damaged by all this beating.

Then we were taken to work. Everybody was going to different places. I happened to be in a group that was taken back to where we had arrived. We worked in a hall with dozens of big bins. When the prisoners arrived, their clothes were taken off. We had to search each garment and look for valuables that people had sewn into their clothes. We would find money, jewelry—diamonds. The Germans took everything. We had to work hard—thousands of people arrived every day.

We had to put the valuables we found in bins. The bins were filled constantly. While working there we could hear people choking from the gas, and children crying. The conditions were indescribable, particularly for a young girl. We worked ten hours a day. We were worried—anxious that we might be the next victims, the next to go into those chambers. We could smell human flesh being burned. There was no chance of escape.

I worked there for many months. We were lice-infected; we had scurvy; we suffered from malnutrition. We women were given a drug so that we did not have periods. We looked like skeletons.

As the Allies were getting closer, they sent us on death marches. By that time we were very weak, and it was winter and cold. We had to march 60 kilometers a day. We had no hair. We had no warm clothing. We had wooden clogs. We were like zombies. You had to do exactly as you were told and keep walking. If you could not keep up with the march, you were just taken out of the row and shot. So not many made it to the destination. If you rebelled, you were shot. If you wanted to live, you did as you were told. It is not that you were a coward. You just had to accept that it was like this. In a way it is a bit like accepting that you grow old. There is no alternative. I don't know where I got the wisdom from. I had no life experience. But I was a fast learner.

Eventually, we arrived at a place called Peterswaldau [Pieszyce] in Lower Silesia in Germany. There was a munitions factory where they made clocks for bombs. After we arrived there, I got scarlet fewer. If the girls had reported that to the SS, that would have been the end. They came on a daily basis to collect the sick people, and the sick never returned. So the girls hid me. And all night they were sponging me with cold water, for there was no medication, and with scarlet fever you have a very high temperature.

In the morning they stood me upright, and they said: 'You are going to march. You are too young to die.' I really did not know what was going on, but I marched with the others to work. At work we were watched by the SS all the time. I worked with a magnifying glass, a *Lupe*, to construct a part of a watch. I pretended to work, and the girls did my part of the work after they had done theirs.

When the sirens sounded, the German citizens were sent to the shelters. Us they sent out into the yard with white handkerchiefs to wave to the planes so that they did not bomb the factory. When I think of it now, that must have been very traumatic. When we were there, we did not think. We just did what we were told. Later I realized that the work at the factory was precise and well planned. The Germans must have worked for many years to perfect it.

One day, after months of working in the factory, we were locked up. We had no idea what was going on. There were 1,000 women at the factory, but only two girls—me and one other. The others tried to protect us as best they could. One of them said, 'There is a white flag hoisted on the city hall. Either they have surrendered, or the war is finished.' After a while the gates were broken down. There was a men's camp some kilometers from Peterswaldau. Men from that camp came up to us, broke down the gates and said, 'Listen, girls, the war is over.' But of course nobody took them seriously. We thought it could be a trick—that the SS wanted us to come out, and that they would then shoot us.

But eventually the men from the other camp managed to convince us, and we went outside. It was 8 May 1945. You know how beautiful May is in Europe. We constantly kept looking behind us, because we were so used to being punished and abused.

It was the Russians who liberated us. It seemed unreal, and it took time before the sensation of being free started to sink in. It was unbelievable. We were used to being constantly hounded. Suddenly it is over, and there is nobody there. What is really going to happen to you? Nobody knows you—nobody really wanted to know much at that stage. It was such an unbelievable experience for the general public. They knew a little, but they had not really spoken to camp survivors.

I was 17, and I simply did not know what was going to happen. The loss and the uncertainty—it was something you cannot possibly imagine. We never had a moment's counseling. You talked to the other survivors, but it was the same sad story. Today when something dramatic happens, you get counseling and support. We had to work through that on our own. I felt so devastated and so lost. It was a frightening experience.

I decided that I would go back to my hometown. I was the sole survivor of my family. But I had a very close girlfriend. Her father was the head of one of the offices that had been established. I said to her, 'I want my birth certificate and other documents there may be about me.' I do not know what made me ask for this. She wondered if her father could manage it. I said, 'Ask him to try'.

And he did. He got me my birth certificate, and he got me my mother's marriage license. That is how I found out how old my mother was. Because, you know, in those days, you never asked your parents to tell you the family's history. Nobody anticipated that anything that tragic would happen. So that is how I found out about my family, including our property in Czechoslovakia. I had felt that I was nobody. I thought, 'Who knows me?' But now I felt that I knew who I was. I just wanted to have an identity. And I needed just that little bit of security.

Eventually we got to Prague. The transport was free, and there were soup kitchens. We sat in a café watching people going by, with the hope of seeing somebody we knew. You might see somebody. There were blackboards where you put your name down, hoping that somebody you knew would see it and know that you had survived.

Then the governments of various foreign countries started to sponsor orphans. There was a quota system: every country had a quota of how many they would take. There were many countries, including Great Britain, Australia and Sweden. I had no idea where Australia was, but I thought it so far away that I wanted to go there. I wanted to get away from those terrible memories and start a new life. So I put my name down for Australia. I wanted to get as far away from Europe as possible.

But there were not many vessels going to Australia. I was sent to a children's home in Paris to wait for a ship that could take us to Australia. We were 61 orphans, mostly boys. The boys went to one home, and I went to another. I was there for six months. The people at the home were kind to us, but it was a difficult period since I could not speak French and therefore could not communicate with them. I left Czechoslovakia on 22 April 1947, and we did not leave Paris until August 1948. I had never seen the sea, so when we arrived in Marseilles and I could hear the roar of the sea, it was such an exciting experience.

The trip took three months. It was a difficult journey with many stops because the ship was not seaworthy and had to be repaired several times. We arrived in Freemantle, Western Australia, on 5 November 1948.

None of us could speak a single word of English. We were divided between different families. But there was no communication, because we could not speak the language. That was quite traumatic, actually. Some stayed in Freemantle, some went to Brisbane, and some to Melbourne. I ended up here in Sydney. We learned English very quickly because we were so motivated—we were in a country that accepted us and gave us an opportunity to start a new life. I shall always be grateful for that. For being able to walk around without anyone abusing you. And for feeling free!

So we started a new life. We worked hard, and we did well. I met my future husband, who is also a child survivor. Seven members of his family were deported from Czechoslovakia, and only he and his brother came back from Auschwitz. We got married on 17 May 1949. We were the first to marry of the child survivors that came to Australia.

I do not know how I survived. I am a very determined person. Maybe I found the strength to survive because I promised my father. Besides, I had faith, and faith helps you in bad times. If you lose faith, there is nothing to hold on to. Many people have lost faith. I never have—not even in Auschwitz. I am a great optimist to this day. Maybe I have never grown up. I never look at the dark side of life but try to look at the bright side. I have always been a positive person. I had tremendous strength. I do not know where I got it from. We were given rations of bread, and each day I would save a piece of bread—in case I would meet my mother. I was very strong—not physically, but mentally. Sometimes mental strength helps a lot. I have seen so much suffering that I am amazed I did not become a bitter person. But I am not.

I had a cousin who had a six-month-old baby. When she got out of the wagon at Auschwitz, she was nursing that child on her arm. She was with her mother, and her mother said, 'Give the baby to me so that you can get some rest.' In that split second when she handed over the baby to her mother, they were sent to the left, and my cousin was sent to the right. Then she felt terrible guilt because she had given her child to her mother, and she suffered from depression both in Auschwitz and after the war. You cannot judge, because everyone copes with their own unhappiness and distress in their own way.

When I speak to school children here at Sydney Jewish Museum, they ask me: 'Do you hate the Germans?' I say, 'No, how come?' Hate is a destructive thing. If I want to heal, I have to not hate. I shall never forget, but I taught my children not to hate. Because it destroys you. We must not forget the six million who perished. The only way we can think they did not perish in vain, is to remember and tell what happened. It was very difficult at the beginning—to come here to the museum every Tuesday and recall all these things. But I felt that since I survived I have got an obligation to keep their memory alive.

The children I talk to are mostly non-Jewish children. They are genuinely interested, and they respond well. They tell me that they will never forget what I tell them. Some of them are younger than I was when it happened. And they can see how fortunate they are not to have lived through anything so terrible. They get a history lesson from a living survivor. The children come here from different parts of Australia. Most of them have never met a Jewish person. They are interested, they are responsive, and that is what we want. We don't want anybody to feel sorry for us. This is living history, which has to be told. Regardless of color, nationality and religion, we are human, and we should respect one another.

The children say to me: 'We have read about the Holocaust, but we do not comprehend. But when we listen to you, that makes an impact and we will remember.' Even if they remember just parts of my story, that is a reward. And the biggest reward, I find, is that they actually listen, and they ask relevant questions.

My husband and I have three children. I was a strict mother. I told them that the most important thing to acquire is an education. Because that is an asset nobody can take from you. Not even the SS could do that. But I also told them that education is not enough. You also have to be a decent human being. That is the most important thing. I am glad I came to Australia. It is wonderful country which has been very kind to us.

I did not talk to my own children about my experience until they were teenagers. How can you tell a five-year-old child that her grandparents perished at Auschwitz? But later I told them. Some years ago members of my family wanted to visit Auschwitz. I was very reluctant—I did not want to go. But I felt that would be selfish—if they wanted to go, we had to go. We saw the museum, with the cases of human hair, suitcases and spectacles taken from the victims. The crematoriums were destroyed, but I could still smell the human flesh. When my husband said a memorial prayer, I felt that was a closure for me. I thought: Here I am. These are my children and my grandchildren, because of me. You have not succeeded in what you set out to do.

Together with Michael, my eldest son, I also went back to the village in the Czech Republic where I lived before the war. The village seemed small compared to what I remembered. Our house is still there. As we stood outside it, Michael said, 'Mum, somebody is calling your name.' I said, 'No, forget it, Michael, that is impossible.' But Michael said, in his quietly insistent way, 'Please, go over and say hello to the lady who is calling your name.' So I did, and the woman asked me, 'Do you remember me?' I said, 'I am sorry, I don't.' 'You sat next to me in school.' I asked, 'How on earth did you recognize me?' She said, 'I would have recognized you anywhere.' That was quite an experience. She recognized me after all those years.

I had an uncle in Czechoslovakia. He told me to remember three things, which I did not quite understand at the time. He was a professional man, a doctor, and he said (it is hard to translate from Czech into English): 'Remember that money is round. Today you have it, tomorrow somebody else. But if you have lost your identity, it is gone forever. And never look at a person's title, but look at what type of human being that person is. Because a title you can acquire if you have the opportunity. But first of all you must be a decent human being. That is what you have to look for in a person.' Now, as I grow older, I understand what he meant.

I am scarred for life, but I cope with it as best I can. I am a happy person. I get great happiness from my children and grandchildren. And life goes on.

In Auschwitz the crematoriums were working 24 hours a day. 6,000 people a day were murdered there. The world knew, but did nothing. If they had bombed the railway lines leading to Auschwitz, the Nazis could not have done what they were doing. You know, one and a half million children perished. These children had no chance in life. When you think of children today, they have all opportunities in life. These children had none. As you get older and think about it, it is really indescribable what you feel.

Yet as survivors we must tell our story. We must try to ensure that this does not happen to anybody else—regardless of religion, color or nationality. We are intelligent human beings. We should be able to tolerate each other. That does not mean we must love each other, but we have to be civil.

Olga Horak

Born on 11 August 1926. Deported to the collection camp Sered in August 1944 and then to Auschwitz. Sent to Kurzbach in October 1944 and then on a death march to Gross-Rosen and Dresden in late December 1944. Sent to Bergen-Belsen in the first days of January 1945 and remained there until the camp was liberated by British and Canadian armed forces on 15 April 1945. Lives in Sydney.

We had a well-functioning democracy in Czechoslovakia before the war. After the First World War, Thomas Garrigue Masaryk created a republic which was a wonderful place to live in. Masaryk had been a professor in the USA before the war, and he married an American lady. He was a fine man, and while he was President, Jewish people had good lives. There was no persecution due to religious differences. Everybody lived in harmony.

But it did not last very long, and things changed rapidly in the 1930s. Before the war broke out, in 1938, Czechoslovakia had to cede what the Germans called Sudetenland to Greater Germany. The central part of the country, where I come from, was made into a self-governing puppet republic called the Slovak Republic. The head of state was Jozef Tiso, a Catholic priest. And he had a pact with Hitler to collect and deport all Jewish people who lived there—never to return. That is very difficult to understand. Because when we did return—a few, not enough—that came as a surprise to the people who thought that Tiso would have succeeded in getting rid of the Jewish population. It is hard to understand today that intelligent people went looting, destroying Jewish homes, stealing and committing criminal offences.

We lived in Bratislava. I was thirteen when the war broke out. Judith, my sister, was 14. My mother, Piroska, was 34 and my father, Hugo Rosenberger, was 45. My father and uncles conducted their livestock business from the family house at Spitalska 45.

Many of my friends and relatives were leaving Slovakia because of the Nuremberg laws. We had to wear the Star of David. I was not ashamed to wear the star, but some people in the street abused me and spat at me. I learned to carry my bag high on my chest to cover the star. We were not allowed to go to school, we were not allowed to sit on a bench in the park, we were not allowed to have businesses or to work, we were not allowed to have non-Jewish friends, and we had to be in our homes after sunset.

These were the initial hardships. I was entering what was supposedly the best part of my life. But we were deprived of the best years of our lives. Unfortunately, the war lasted for six years. That was too long, and it was hard to accept that a whole generation of middle-aged people and old people were killed. Only some of the young ones survived, by miracle or their faith. I do not believe in miracles, but I believe in faith.

So I could not go to school. But my parents were well off, and we had private tutors teaching us English and French and other subjects, like handicraft. There was a lot we had to endure, but I am jumping now to 1942. At that time my sister Judith was sixteen and a half, and I was one year younger. Suddenly a law was introduced that said that all Jewish boys and girls aged sixteen were to be collected and taken away. Because it was supposedly high time the Jews learned how to work.

Anyway, Judith was on the list. The guards came to our home after sunset, collected her, took her away, and we never saw her again. It is terrible when you have to repeat words like 'collection'— 'collection of Jewish people'. Because nobody collects people—you collect art, you collect stamps or whatever. Thus, this idea of collecting people was hard to understand.

My parents were beside themselves when my sister was taken away. They did all they could to protect me, because I could easily enough have been on the list not long after. My father had an old friend who was a minister in Tiso's government at that time, and he always offered to help. 'Whenever you need anything, just come to me and we will talk things over,' he said. My father never needed any help. He was a proud man and a loyal citizen.

That was the only time he remembered the offer. My father went to this man and begged him: 'Please, help me, my child has been taken away.' He said, 'I cannot do anything for you.' My father came back, and he cried. He was disappointed.

This is how people changed, without any reason whatsoever. Overnight you became a stranger, you were an enemy, you had to be despised—just because you were Jewish. When this happened, we could not find a hiding place. They were hard to find. Hiding places were offered by some people— sometimes for money but in a few cases without asking to be paid. That did not happen often, but I mention it because good people should not be forgotten. If we don't mention the good people, we lose faith in humankind, and that would be wrong.

We were desperate after Judith's deportation, and shortly afterwards my parents made the decision to flee to Hungary. One day in late spring in 1942 we were ready. Guided by a peasant, we—I, my parents and some other members of my family—crossed the border illegally.

When we came to Budapest, a relative met us and handed my parents Hungarian money and coupons to buy food. We had no documents and no work. We pretended to be from the country, and said we were visiting Budapest because my father needed medical treatment. Fortunately, we spoke some Hungarian. We stayed in different apartments. While my father stayed indoors, Mother went shopping.

The winter of 1943 was very cold, but somehow we managed to get through it. In the spring of 1944 the political situation got worse: Germany occupied Hungary. With the German army came the Gestapo and the SS. Suddenly the attitude changed, and Jews in hiding were denounced. Caretakers in apartment buildings were now appointed as spies and were paid by the KEOKH [Külfödieket Ellenőrző Erszágos Központi Hatósá] [National Central Alien Control Office] when they denounced 'illegal' Jews. We heard that people who were arrested were 'sent to Poland' or 'sent to Auschwitz'. Although I did not fully understand what that meant, it was enough to make me afraid. Life was very tense. We never knew if someone would recognize us. We never knew what questions would be asked.

One day we were warned by our caretaker that a search would take place within a few minutes. We were grateful for the warning, but we were also desperate. We left the place at once and never returned. My mother took my father to the Jewish Hospital. One of the nurses was the daughter of an old friend. Father pretended to be very sick, and she protected him. My mother and I now had no place to stay. We sought shelter wherever we could find it. It was an impossible situation. We were like hunted animals.

Since the situation in Hungary was worsening every day, my parents believed it would be better for us to return to Slovakia. After all, Bratislava was home, and it was familiar. Aunt Aranka and Uncle Jakob agreed, and together with their son Thomas they prepared to join us. As my father was relatively safe in the hospital, he was able to contact people in Bratislava and plan our return.

The return trip was tense. At the Keleti station [the main railway station in Budapest] we boarded the train to the border village. The Hungarian gendarmes were on the platform of the station checking papers and travel documents. We had neither and prayed silently that we would get through. My parents and I were not stopped, but Aunt Aranka and Uncle Jakob were arrested and taken away. Their fifteen-year-old son followed us. My aunt and uncle vanished. They were deported to Auschwitz, and we never saw them again. Thomas never spoke about his parents again.

Our guide took us from the village to the forest. We walked through the night and eventually crossed the border into Slovakia. We managed to board a train for Bratislava and arrived home at Spitalska 45. We were physically and mentally exhausted.

The house was still there, along with many members of the Rosenberger family. But there were also the painful memories of those who had been deported. We knew nothing about them. I tried to get in touch with some of my old friends. Greta Fischer, who was my age, had joined the partisans, but I was unable to contact her. Other friends had either disappeared or had gone into hiding.

Although life was hard, we were still together as a family, and we were still in our home. However, in late August 1944 an uprising against the Tiso regime broke out in Central Slovakia. The Germans used the uprising as an excuse to invade and occupy the country. As always, the Gestapo and the SS were not far behind.

Shortly after the Germans marched in, deportations resumed. Our parents were convinced that we had to go into hiding. Now, my mother had a good friend. She was a pharmacist, and she was our next-door neighbour. Mrs. Chmelar had two apartments, one behind her pharmacy, and a different one. She came to my mother and said: 'You cannot stay here. Here are the keys to my apartment. Take your essentials and move in. I will be your contact person, and I will look after you.'

That was unheard-of, and we gratefully accepted and moved to her apartment. What then happened is difficult to explain, even today. Two weeks later this lady, our Good Samaritan, brought the guards to the apartment and denounced us. You know, that was such a disappointment—in people. I have no explanation for why she did it. This was in August 1944. They took us away to the collection camp, Sered. I was still with my parents. Collection camps were usually erected close to a railway line in a village. However, people in Sered would have known about the camp, since the guards lived in the village.

Once the camp was overcrowded, in a couple of weeks, they took us out from the barracks to the railway line. There were the carriages waiting for us—cattle carriages—and we were pushed in. This is the way we were transported to Auschwitz. You have probably seen a cattle carriage. What it is made for? To transport horses or cows. How many horses or how many cows are you permitted to transport in one carriage? There is actually an international law: you are permitted to transport eight horses or eight cows or forty people. We were pushed in up to one hundred in one carriage. You have no idea how horrible the situation was. We were packed together like sardines. Not only that, there were elderly people, people had heart attacks, people screamed, and people suffocated and died.

How long it took us to reach Auschwitz, I cannot tell you. For once you are confined in a dark place, you lose your sense of timing. The doors were bolted from the outside. Inside it was horrible. We had no food or water. There was just one bucket which served for necessity. I was a young, modest girl. I could not use it. It was a horrible feeling.

When we arrived at Auschwitz, the transport of the human cargo stopped. We did not know where we were. They unbolted the doors, and the guards were shouting and screaming. You know, when they scream *Schnell, schnell! Raus, raus!* ('Quickly! Quickly! Out! Out!') I did not know *why* we had to be *schnell*. What was the hurry for? There was something sick in their minds.

Auschwitz was a city in Poland before the war, during the war, and after the war. People lived there then, and they live there now. I have seen it—I went back to Auschwitz six years ago. I was with a film crew that made a documentary. The camp was virtually round the corner from the city. The fact is that people living in the city of Auschwitz did not admit to have known about the horrible camp that was there. But the camp existed, it was vast, and some of the people who lived in the city even worked inside the camp. So it is very hard to believe that people did not know about it. I cannot accept that. Not only must they have known because they saw it, but the stench from the burning of the bodies lingered in the air for twenty-four hours, day and night. So it is impossible to deny what happened there. This kind of denial is also something that I find hard to explain.

We knew nothing about Auschwitz when the train stopped there. We had read about Poland, including the capital[, Warsaw,] and the main industries, but not about Auschwitz. This is how it was a surprise. Those who were very weak and dead had to be taken out of the carriages. From the ramp by the train I could see the part of the camp which I now know was Birkenau. We were ordered to separate. Men had to form one line, women another. There was a third line for women with children, elderly, and sick people. I was together with my mother.

At the ramp I could also see women prisoners dressed in leather jackets and leather boots. They wore armbands with the word KAPO. I saw one of these prisoners using a whip on some of the prisoners who had just arrived. I stopped breathing. It was someone I knew, Eta. She had been in the same class as Judith and had been on the first transport with my sister in March 1942. I was disgusted at what I saw and shouted, 'Eta, what are you doing?' Hearing her name, she turned round, looked at me and recognized me. Then she said, 'Olly, believe me, I am not a human anymore. I am an animal.' I did not see Eta again in Auschwitz, but I met her many months later in Bergen-Belsen.

I also saw another woman I knew, Mrs Fischer. She had owned a restaurant in Bratislava before the war. Mrs Fischer recognized my mother and came over to us. 'Mrs Rosenberger,' she whispered to my mother, 'listen carefully. Never volunteer for anything!' Then she gave my mother a small piece of carrot and said, 'And remember: this is a piece of gold.'

There were many SS men waiting on the arrival ramp. They were dressed in immaculate black uniforms and polished boots. One of the SS men sat behind a table. He was in charge of the process of selecting people: sorting out people who were taken to the gas chambers shortly after arriving. He was a young, handsome man. I remember that he wore leather gloves. He was Dr Josef Mengele, the 'Angel of Death'.

We had never heard about Mengele until we arrived at Auschwitz. Later I learned that Mengele had his own laboratory in Auschwitz where he committed horrible experiments, removing the private parts of men, sterilizing women, and so on. He took a particular interest in twins and dwarfs. He collected people for his laboratory after the prisoners arrived. We were sorted into three groups, and then we were told that '*Doktor* Mengele is going to make a *Selektion*.' What is 'selection'? What do you select? You select items when you go shopping, not people. But that is exactly what he did.

I stood in the line with other women. Immediately behind me were my aunt Franziska and her daughter Ruth. Father stood with his sisters and their children in a different line. Suddenly they were led away. There was no time to say anything. They were gone.

As the line I was in approached the table where Mengele sat, we were ordered to strip completely naked. That was a great shock. It was degrading and humiliating. I was young and would not have undressed in front of anybody. But that was what we had to do. Now we had to form a single line and walk towards Mengele, who looked at us, deciding who was young and fit enough to be sent to the right. Anyone who was not considered good enough by Mengele was sent to the left. Those sent to the left could also be young and healthy, but maybe they had a scar or some insignificant mark. They were not 'perfect'. So we never knew what to expect.

I approached the table. Mengele looked me up and down like a butcher inspecting meat, and waved me to the right. My mother was a healthy, well-developed woman. She was shown to the right as well. I was 16 ½, and my mother 39. We had passed the first *Selektion* at Auschwitz.

My cousin Ruth, who was 15, was sent to our side, and then aunt Franziska stood before Mengele. She had a scar due to an abdominal operation; Mengele sent her to the left. Ruth immediately walked back to the table and pleaded for her mother: 'Please, let my mother be with me.' Mengele stood up and slapped Ruth hard across the face. Then he showed aunt Franziska to the right. It seemed like a miracle! Ruth had saved her mother. Both women survived the war.

After the *Selektion* the column on the left moved in one direction, while we on the right were marched to a large hall. The Kapos yelled orders at us, beating those who did not move quickly enough. In the hall we were shaved and deloused by inmates. These privileged prisoners were both women and men. I found the shaving even more humiliating than standing naked before Mengele. The woman who shaved me had a sarcastic grin on her face. She first cut off my curly shoulder-length hair. Then my armpits were shaved, and then my pubic hair. The clippers were so blunt that I bled from the shaven areas.

A different prisoner then dipped a mop into a bucket full of carbolic liquid and smeared it over my shaven head, under my arms and between my legs. Why did we need to be 'disinfected'? We were civilized, cultured, clean—we did not come from a slum. This was part of the picture the Nazis painted of us—that we were 'dirty'. 'You dirty Jew', 'You bloody Jew'—this attitude was ingrained in them. It was a sort of motto they repeated.

That was our welcome to Auschwitz. Then we were given old rags to cover our bodies with. Instead of shoes we were given wooden clogs. We were also numbered. A prisoner painted a number on my back and over my left breast. Many prisoners were tattooed—some on the inside of their arms, some on the outside. I was not tattooed. Thousands of people arrived every day, and there was not enough time to tattoo every prisoner.

Then we marched to the barracks. I think I was in the *B Lager*. Inside were three-tier beds covered with bits of dirty straw. Two to four women shared one narrow bunk. Near the entrance there was a small room, separated with a blanket. This was the room of our *Stubova* (or *Stubenälteste*). This privileged prisoner was in charge of the inmates in our barracks.

Twice a day we were taken out for roll call. At 4am in the morning and 5pm in the afternoon the *Stubova* would start shouting, ordering us out of the barracks. The roll call was a torture. We had to stand motionless until the SS were satisfied with the counting. Sometimes people collapsed with exhaustion. Even the dead were dragged out so that the numbers tallied.

I was one of the youngest in my group. I was not selected for hard manual work in Auschwitz, but I had to help carrying the drums of soup from one place to another. Each prisoner was given a dish of soup at night. In the morning we were given a small tin mug with *Ersatzkaffee* (a substitute coffee made from chicory), which was really black water, and a small slice of black bread. When queuing for the soup, it was important to find the right place in the line. If you hurried and were among the first, all you got was murky hot water. If you were too slow and were at the end of the line, there might be no soup left at all. But if you were in the centre of the line, there would be enough soup left in the drum and it was still warm and thick. I learnt these tricks quickly. It was a matter of survival.

After the war I learnt that the food was probably poisoned. The 'coffee' and soup were laced with bromide. Bromide stopped menstruation, which in reality was a blessing since we had no sanitary measures. But our systems were badly affected, and most of us did not function normally for many years after Liberation. This also happened to me.

As the days in the camp went by, I became like my fellow prisoners. We were lethargic and generally disinterested. When someone remarked that it was Rosh Hashanah or Yom Kippúr, the Jewish High Holy Days, we did not react. Emotions had died within us. If they did not, the pain from what was happening to us would have been too much to bear. It was better not to let yourself feel anything, just try to stay alive for another day.

After many weeks in the camp there was a sudden change. I was still with my mother. One morning after roll call we were told not to return to the barracks. We were marched into an open space. Here we had to await *Selektion*. Mengele came, 'inspected' us, and selected most of us for hard labour. I think we were about 200 women. Waiting for further orders, we had to remain standing until the evening. We stood for what seemed like days. We were given no food. Many collapsed and fell to the ground where they lay unaided. I fell asleep, cradled in my mother's lap.

Suddenly there was shouting. Along with the Kapos, SS men and SS women ordered us into lines, counted us, and then marched us off. At this point I did not care anymore. I just walked with the rest of the group, with my mother beside me. We arrived at a ramp outside the *Lager*. There was an old locomotive and the familiar sight of the cattle wagons. Loaded aboard and sealed in our carriages, we felt the train starting to move. We had no idea where the train was taking us. But really, we did not care as long as it was away from Auschwitz.

We passed through towns and villages, and finally we arrived at a tiny place named Kurzbach. There were just a few cottages, which were occupied by the Nazi guards. Kurzbach was deep inside a forest. We were taken to a straw barn with no floor, but there were three-tier bunks that we had to sleep in. It was very cold. We had to get up at five and stand at roll-call where we were counted. Counted and counted—what a sick idea! Look, who would have helped us? We were visibly inmates from camps—shaven heads, rags, numbers … You know, the population there saw us. They cannot deny that they saw us.

From the barn we had to march ten kilometers to a forest to work. We had to dig trenches for the Nazi army. They were not narrow trenches for soldiers. They were huge pits—either they were anti-tank trenches, or they were trenches where they were hiding armaments because we had to cover it with foliage. That is what we had to do. We had no food at work. We were hardly covered with anything—just rags. In winter it was unbearable. And we women—we had to dig trenches in frozen ground. It was very hard work.

In the evening we had to march back to the barn. We were tortured on the way. We had to lie down in the snow and do push ups. That was cruel. What is significant to mention is that we did not only have male guards. We had female guards too. They did not show compassion in any way. What sort of human being cannot show compassion at certain times? It is hard for me to understand. People say women have softer attitudes. I have not seen it. And it is very disappointing. Because I believe in the goodness of people. And when you are young you have ideals.

We were at Kurzbach until the end of December 1944. One morning, instead of marching to work we were told to march onto the highway. That was the beginning of the death march. We had no communication—no radios or newspapers. Nobody talked to us. But as we were walking through villages, we saw Christmas trees through the windows, so we realized it must be Christmas time. We also realized that we were being evacuated, and that Allied forces must be approaching from different sides.

We had to march on. I do not know how many days we marched. I was still with my mother. She had not given up hope of finding Father or Judith. My mother's strength kept me alive.

We arrived at the camp Gross-Rosen. But the camp was so overcrowded that after the third day it was decided that we should continue marching. Towards evening we arrived in a village square. Our first ration in days was distributed—watery soup and a small slice of black bread. Close to us the SS were eating too. Their hot pea soup smelt of smoked meat and that smell lingered in my nose. It is strange that after all these years I have no memory of how far I marched, but I can remember what the SS ate in the village square that evening.

The march continued. If we were tired and could not walk anymore and had to sit down, the SS would shoot us on the spot. I often ask myself: what made us go on? Where did we find the strength? How was it possible still to believe in God? I cannot explain it. However, we still hoped that one day it would all be over. But many of the women I marched with never saw that day.

Then we came to Dresden. We arrived in the city itself, and the death march seemed to be over. We were pushed into open train trucks made for carrying timber. It was unbearably cold. Huddled together, we tried to stay as warm as we could in the freezing wind.

In Dresden we witnessed a big air raid. During the raid, we watched as the bombs fell like manna from heaven. Our 'brave' SS guards ran towards the shelters and left us in the open. We could not escape. We were too sick, and nobody would have helped us in any case. Miraculously, our train was not hit. After the raid our guards returned. The train started to move, and we were taken to Bergen-Belsen.

We were given no food or water during the journey. The train travelled through Weimar, Halle and Hannover. Since we were in open carriages we could read the names on the station buildings. Many of us died during the journey. But because of the intense cold, and because we were packed together, they somehow had remained upright, frozen stiff among the living. When the train stopped at Bergen-Belsen, they were pulled out with the rest of us.

We were now very sick. My body fat had disappeared months ago. My bones stuck out, my breasts had all but disappeared, my teeth were loose in my mouth. My eyes were sunken in their sockets, the little hair I had was patchy, and I could barely stand upright. Yet I was not as sick as the inmates I saw in Bergen-Belsen.

Bergen-Belsen is a city—a pretty city. People lived there before, during and after the war. Actually, after liberation, the mayor of the city said he did not know about the camp, and the British made him and his colleagues come into the camp to see it, and to prove that it existed. This is hard to believe even today. How can they deny a fact like this?

The camp, Bergen-Belsen, was vast, stretching for kilometers. It was similar to Auschwitz. The only difference was that they did not have gas chambers. But they had crematoriums, and they had open pits where they burnt the bodies day and night, non-stop. So the stench was beyond description.

Along with my mother, I was directed to a *Schälküche*, the peeling kitchen. Here we had to peel big turnips with blunt knives. It was forbidden to eat any of the turnips or the peels. It was yet another torture to have to peel the turnips and not be able to hide even a few scraps to eat later on. However, I had been in the camps long enough to know what would happen if I was caught. And now I was determined to survive.

Yet one day my hunger overcame me. I was working in the *Schälküche* when I noticed a turnip peel on the floor. I *had* to have it. I reached to grab it, but a guard saw me and stabbed me in my arm with his bayonet. I did not scream, just tried to ignore the horrible pain. I still have the scar.

My health continued to decline. My mother and I caught typhus almost immediately. The acute diarrhoea, vomiting and dehydration made us too weak to move. Others suffered from tuberculosis and cholera. Outside the barracks there were piles of bodies waiting to be 'processed'. The stench was unbelievable.

In the final weeks before the liberation conditions in the camp got even worse. The bread ration was reduced to less than a slice a day. Then it stopped, and our only food was a cup of soup. Then the water stopped—for nearly a week there was no drinking water for the prisoners. At this point our morale was completely broken. I believed we were all dying. We had no news of the war, and we had no idea where the nearest Allied troops were.

We were in Bergen-Belsen from January 1945 until we were liberated on 15 April. On that day we were standing for roll call in the morning, waiting for the SS guards to count us. But they never arrived. Then, suddenly, we saw tanks and heard shooting. We noticed that these soldiers were not Germans, but from a different army. We realized we were liberated. Of course we found out later that it was the British army together with the Canadian forces.

These forces had no idea what was waiting for them. They had come into Germany to fight the war, to win the war. When they saw the camp and saw the *Muselmänner*, as we were called—walking skeletons—they were scared of us. Not only because of the terrible shock, for they had never seen anything like this. They were scared of us because we were highly infectious by then. We were covered in lice—big lice, not head lice. They were eating us alive and were the best conductors of infectious disease. These big lice arrived with the Soviet army.

The British soldiers retreated for a few hours. Then they brought DDT and we were decontaminated and deloused with the white powder. DDT is forbidden now because it is dangerous, but it was a blessing to be relieved of the plague of the lice.

The next morning we had to line up to register. A makeshift tent was set up, and at the table in the tent was an officer. We had to tell him our names, where we came from and where we wanted to be repatriated to. In order to be registered, we received tiny little cards. My mother came in front of the table. She gave her information. She received her card. She collapsed. I lost her; she did not make it.

My mother is registered as a survivor. She is not counted as a victim. I was behind her, and of course I was devastated. My mother had survived Auschwitz, Kurzbach, the death march to Dresden, and four months in Bergen-Belsen—only to die just after being registered as a survivor. I had lost her. My mother was 40 years old, and I was 18. Now I was completely alone.

I was registered. A few days later I was found half dead in front of the barracks. I was taken away; they tried to help me, but they had limited medical equipment. What the army had was for themselves, not for survivors. A sick bay was improvised—there were some stretchers and clean sheets. But they did not know what to do with me. When the nurses weighed me, I was 29 kilos.

They transferred me to Celle, which is a city not far from Bergen-Belsen. There was a big public hospital. It was a German hospital, and it was still war. All the beds were occupied by sick Germans. I was the only Jewish person in the hospital. The German nurses did not want to look after me. They did not clean me. They did not give me food. They placed me in a corner of a large ward and left me there to die.

I was very sick, but my mind was as clear as crystal. I knew something was going on, and I was fighting it. I was very lucky. In every army they have priests and clergymen from different denominations to look after the wounded and dying. One morning a British officer in uniform, a Catholic priest, came to visit the sick in the hospital. He did not come specifically to visit me, but when he saw me in the corner of the ward, he came to my bed. He had a crucifix in his hand and a prayer book, and he wanted to give me the last rites. He had no idea who I was.

I looked at him and I said, 'Sorry, Padre.' I was lucky that I spoke English. 'You cannot give me the last rites, because I am Jewish. And I am not going to die.'

The priest looked at me. He was totally surprised, and he asked, 'What can I do for you?' I said, 'Have you got a rabbi in your army?' He said, 'Yes.' And I said, 'Please return to your unit. Bring the rabbi and a stretcher. Because the German nurses still believe that Hitler will win the war, and they don't want to look after a Jewish patient.'

And that's exactly what happened. Within a few hours they came with an open jeep. The jeep was covered with the Red Cross flag. There were the Rabbi and the Padre, both in British uniforms. They took me out of the German hospital, returned me to the sick bay in the camp, and there I was kept till the end of the war in the Pacific area. That was in August. Then they destroyed the camp because it was infectious. But still I think it was wrong to destroy Bergen-Belsen, thus removing proof of the crimes committed there.

I was put on a military hospital train and finished up at the state hospital of Pilzen, in the western part of Czechoslovakia. They were not expecting patients as sick as we were, but the nurses were wonderful. They were Roman Catholic nuns—highly dedicated women and the best nurses, who were very kind to us. One of them, an elderly nun with a kind, smiling face, put me in a small private room. A patient in that room had just died of tuberculosis, and she said I could use that patient's bed. I said, 'No, thank you.' Instead I sat down in a wicker armchair that stood in the corner. I covered myself with my blanket—I had a blanket made of human hair—and fell asleep.

I stayed in that chair for the next three days and nights, until my turn came to be taken to the X-ray room to establish whether I had tuberculosis. I actually had not. I was put in a ward with women who suffered from sexually transmitted diseases after having been raped. It was not just the Russians who raped women—soldiers from the Allied forces did so too. The only ones in the ward who did not have venereal disease were I and the woman next to me. She was a hairdresser, and she had eczema due to chemicals she had been using.

This woman took me to her place. She was a poor, divorced woman. She had just one room, and she kept me there. I could not get up, so she locked the door in the morning, went to work, and brought me food and milk—whatever she could get on the black market. I stayed there until I was strong enough to get out of bed and stand on my feet. I had never seen this woman before. That was a good human being. She is not alive anymore, but her daughter is. I still support her daughter financially, because she is in need.

So I do not forget the good people. I do not forget the bad either. Maybe the bad experience has made a greater impact. I must have had good times in my childhood. But the hardships and the losses have had such a terrible impact. That may be why we now talk about the experiences from the war.

Yet for a long time we did not talk. In a way I think that is normal. Besides, when we came here [to Australia] we had to start a new life. I consider myself as being born again in this country. And I had to bring up a family—that was my desire, and it was not the time to tell sad stories.

After Pilzen I was repatriated and went back to Bratislava. I found our house, but there was no homecoming: I was the sole survivor of our family. But I also found lovely people who, like me, had been repatriated and who were survivors of Theresienstadt. They were second cousins of my grandmother. They took me in, and I stayed with them till I got married in 1947.

Shortly after Czechoslovakia had political changes [in 1948], my husband said to me, 'We are not staying here.' My husband had a friend who managed to obtain passports for us. It was difficult to obtain a passport if you were not a member of the Communist party, which we were not. We managed to make contact with the Swiss consul, who managed to get us a visa. Then we could travel, legally, to Zürich. But, and this is a sore point for me, we were not allowed to stay on a permanent basis.

By this time Palestine was no longer an option for us. Before I got married I could perhaps have ended up on a kibbutz, but not now. We were waiting for permission to go to the United States, or Canada, where I had relatives. However, you had to wait for a very long time. So we ended up staying in Switzerland for eleven months. Then we decided we would go to Australia. We were screened and interviewed, and eventually we got the landing permit—and came to Sydney.

That was a good choice. My husband was a textile engineer, and his degree was not acknowledged [in Australia]. So we established a textile factory within two weeks of arriving. I had no training for that kind of work, but I had bought a small sewing machine in Switzerland, and I was ready to start something with my husband in his profession. We produced blouses only, because I could not make dresses. We were quite successful.

Then, of course, I wanted to have a family. I have two daughters and three grandchildren and one great-grandchild—who was born yesterday [2013]. Our children were born in a different atmosphere. It was not a normal household. We could not talk about our hardship; I am sure we behaved differently. When I squeeze an orange, I make sure it is squeezed until the very last drop.

When children are small, you read fairytales to them and talk about *Little Red Riding Hood*, not about Auschwitz. Later the children started to ask questions. 'Why don't we have a grandma?' 'Why don't we have aunts, cousins, uncles?' So gradually, we had to explain. And once we started to talk, perhaps we talked too much. It was difficult.

I remember that one time one of my daughters said to me: 'We know it all. Live for the future, don't live in the past.' I said, 'I don't live in the past. The past lives in me.' That is the difference.

People could not escape from Auschwitz. Auschwitz was surrounded by fences that were charged with high-voltage electricity. If you touched the fence, you were gone. There were very few who committed suicide. This is hard to believe, because under conditions like this you sometimes think: why continue? This is important to mention to young people, who sometimes feel that they cannot cope and that they have to end their lives. But under the conditions we were in Auschwitz very few people took their own lives. That is significant, because hope played a very important role. We hoped that one day this would be over.

I am glad to be of use here at the Sydney Jewish Museum. There is still the possibility to question me, while I am alive. Of course we are fewer now who are active as guides at the museum than when we started, because we are an aging group. Now some are in nursing homes and so on. Earlier we had a very active group of survivors here—though we came from different cultures and different countries. And from different camps, with different feelings. The reactions to how we behaved then were also different. The behavior of men and women was also different, even though they were in the same camp.

If people listen to my story, then I am glad. We need to leave a legacy. Once we are gone, people will read just a few lines in a book by some historian. There will be very little information. Those of us who are still active as guides here make sure that all information is correct—those who listen to us get it straight from the horse's mouth.

I speak to different people here at the museum. They are mostly good people who are grateful to learn more about the Holocaust. But I have encountered some difficult situations. Some of our visitors are German. I recognize their accent and can speak to them in German. A German man reacted strongly to something I said. I asked, 'Have I offended you?' He said, 'No, it is just that I would not have expected to be talked to by a Holocaust survivor.' However, you cannot condemn young people for the deeds of their parents. Although I still have scars deep inside me, I do not carry hatred within me.

I am introduced as a Holocaust survivor. Many visitors have no idea what that is—are we green with little horns? They cannot understand it. Nor can they understand the fact that being Jewish is your religion: you do not necessarily look different. My father was blonde and blue-eyed, and he was Jewish. There is no way to make a stereotype out of anybody. This is what

131

we have to explain. We, the survivors, cannot forget the Holocaust. Not only those who were in the camps are survivors, there are also many others. My husband was on the run for three years. His father was deported to Auschwitz and perished there, but John managed to run away—and survived. John passed away in 2008. That gives me another reason for being active here, rather than to be lonely at home.

Zdenka Fantlová

Born on 28 March 1922. Deported to Theresienstadt in January 1942. In the autumn of 1944 sent to Auschwitz, and later to Kurzbach. Sent from Kurzbach on a death march to Gross Rosen, and then on a train to Mauthausen and Bergen-Belsen, where she remained until the liberation of the camp on 15 April 1945. Lives in London.

I had a happy childhood at home. We lived civilized lives—like most people do. It was a peaceful family life with father, mother, sister, brother, grandfather and grandmother. It consisted of school, holidays, love affairs, skating—and making plans for the future. So it was an idyllic life.

We lived in Rokycany, a town in the western part of the Czechoslovak Republic. My father had his iron brokerage, and he spent all week travelling. But he could not wait to get back to his beloved Betty and his children. There were not many Jewish families in Rokycany, but they were well integrated into the life of the town. So was our family. We did not feel superior or inferior to the rest.

Grandfather observed all the Jewish holidays scrupulously. My father and mother kept the holidays too. My only objection to the Jewish holidays was that I was not allowed to go to school on those days and had to wear my best clothes even though it was a weekday. This made me feel excluded. My schoolmates stared at me as if they had never seen me before. It was as if I did not belong among them, even though I was the same person I was the day before. Broadly, however, life went on in a calm, peaceful way.

Of course, we knew what was happening in Germany. The radio had broadcast several of the demagogic speeches given by the new Chancellor, one Adolf Hitler. I remember my mother was listening to the broadcast—with Hitler raging and his audience crying *Sieg Heil!* and so on. But my father said, 'Don't listen to the radio. That is Germany. We have our own nation, our own freedom, our own government. President Masaryk is in charge here, and no country in the world has a better leader.' In those days, Germany was far away.

Then, one morning, on 15 March 1939, my father woke us up: 'Quick, quick! Come to the window!' We drew the curtains open. And there was the German invasion: men on motorcycles, in strange uniforms and with helmets, driving past our house. It was a frightening sight. The motorized columns came in hundreds from the west, passing through our city and heading towards Prague. It was a total surprise. On the radio there was a voice telling the public to remain calm and warning against any form of resistance.

How do you react to a political situation when you are seventeen? Personally, for me, the best news of the day was that there was to be no school. In a complex political situation you react to what is closest to you. And that goes right through the four years of concentration camps. Excuse my jumping ahead. The details of the occupation are now history—how people were put on a list, how we had to give up many things, even domestic animals. In the immediate situation, how do you explain to a dog that looks at you with sad eyes: 'You can't stay with us anymore, because we are Jews.' Life is turned upside down. There are immense changes, upheavals that have not been caused by you personally. And yet they influence your life, in my case changing it forever.

So Germany took over our country. The Nuremberg laws were implemented. My father got a note from school: 'According to new laws, your daughter, Zdenka Fantlová, is not allowed to attend our institute as of today because of her Jewish background.' So I was out. And it did not make sense. Surprisingly, you react normally to abnormal conditions. This is the paradox. People would say: 'This is stupid. They will change their mind, and you will come back.' Well, in reality, it was stupid, but they did not change their mind, and I could not come back to school.

And then something happened which I believe was a combination of fate and our free will. Our free will makes us think we can change things— sometimes it works, sometimes it does not. But the blueprint that we have—I believe, from the minute we are born—is there. Fate is a kind of blueprint. Little things of no importance interfere suddenly and change the course of your life.

At the time, they made a film in Hollywood, a musical called *Broadway Melody*, which had no connection with me whatsoever. I did not even know where Hollywood was and had no interest in this film at all. But my cousin Bedrich came with a disc, and he said, 'I always have the first things that appear. Here is a record with Fred Astaire from the new Hollywood film, *Broadway Melody*, would you like to hear it?' I was not interested at all, but not to offend him I said, 'Yes.' This was in the days of the old gramophone. You had to wind it up and drop the needle. There was this sexy voice singing. I did not understand a word, but somehow I was fascinated. And I decided I must learn English. I had no reason whatsoever. At home we spoke Czech, and I did not know a single soul in England. And yet, listening to that song I felt, almost like a premonition, that I had to learn English, come what may.

As it happened, this language saved my life. And this is what I call a blueprint because at the time, English seemed to be of no use to me at all. There was an English Institute in Prague where no race laws applied. They took anyone who wanted to learn English. Once I had decided that I must learn the language, I managed to persuade my father to send me there. I was delighted when he agreed! In Prague I stayed with Grandmother, who lived close to the Old Town Square. I loved the sound of English, worked hard and tried to be the best student. I became friends with Marta, a student who sat next to me, and who had also been expelled from school on racial grounds. We used to go on trips outside Prague. We would take the yellow star off our coats and walk into forbidden areas, not returning home until after 8pm, when Jewish people were not even allowed on the streets. We both passed our exams with distinction.

After Prague life at home seemed empty and boring. The people of our town polarized into two camps. Some spurned the German regulations and secretly helped us. But others started collaborating with the Germans, spying on us and denouncing us in return for promises and rewards from them. At that time we had to give up our radios. There was the 'danger' that we might hear something that was not comfortable for the Germans. Listening to the BBC was strictly forbidden—if caught you would be severely punished for doing that. A neighbour came over to us and asked my father, 'Would you like to come to my home and listen to the BBC? Jan Masaryk is going to broadcast from London.' My father, who was a true patriot, went to listen to Masaryk's speech. He came back excited.

Soon after, one evening there was a knock on the door: *Gestapo! Aufmachen!* 'Open up!' Somebody who knew that Father had listened to the BBC had denounced him. Three SS men burst in, shouting *Achtung! Aufstehen!* 'Attention! Stand up!' One of them shook my father and cried, 'Name?' Father answered calmly with the German pronunciation of his name: 'Ernst Fantl'. *Was?* 'What?' the SS man shouted, and then told Father how he *should* have answered: 'Jew, Ernst Fantl!' —and hit him again. Then the officer in charge said to Father: *Jetzt kommst du mit uns!* 'Now you come with us!' Father was very calm, concentrated, and before leaving the room he turned round, looked intently for a moment at each of us in turn as if to remember us, and then said in a low but steady voice, 'Just keep calm. Remember, calmness is strength.' And he raised his hat to us in silent farewell. The SS men slammed the door, and Father disappeared from sight.

This sentence, 'Calmness is strength', sank deep into my subconscious and carried me right through the war. In every critical situation I said to myself, 'Stay calm.' And he was so right.

Because of the German invasion, Jewish families in the Sudeten borderland had begun to move inland. One family who moved into our town had a son whose name was Arnošt, the same name as that of my father. Arnošt was a striking young man with dark hair and brown eyes that looked straight at you. He was 23. We fell in love immediately. We met as often as we could, often wandering in the woods. Arno, as I called him, used to come up to our window and whistle the theme from [Antonin] Dvořák's *New World Symphony*, our signature tune. I always dropped everything immediately and ran outside to him. We could see nothing but one another and felt no danger lurking ahead. Even the German occupation vanished from our horizon. We felt that love would overcome all obstacles.

In the autumn of 1941 we started to hear rumours from Prague. According to these rumours, lists were being drawn up of Jewish families who were to be transported 'to the East'. Where in 'the East'? No one knew. But there is no smoke without fire, and the rumours turned out to be true.

The name Terezín (Theresienstadt to the Germans) meant little to us at the time. It was very convenient for the Germans to send most of the Jews to Terezín, because it was a walled town.

In November 1941 the first two transports to Terezín left Prague. They consisted of 2,000 young men who were to do construction work to prepare Terezín for the many Jews who were going to be sent there. My cousin

Bedrich, who had introduced me to the Fred Astaire number 'You Are My Lucky Star', was on the first transport.

Our turn came sooner than we had expected. In early January 1942 we were summoned to a large nearby town to be registered. There was a great crowd assembled from the whole area. We stood in a row, facing the uniformed Germans sitting behind tables. We stepped forward, gave our name and were given a narrow slip of paper with a transport number. My heart was beating with fear that Arno should be sent somewhere different from me. He and his family were in the row in front of me, and it turned out that their transport had the letter R. I was trembling to know what mine would be. I and my family were assigned to transport S. My worst fear had become reality: Arno and I would be separated. The crowd was tense and noisy, and the Germans were shouting to speed things up.

Transport R was to leave on 16 January 1942; destination unknown. Perhaps the train was bound for Terezín, perhaps for somewhere else. I was full of apprehension. Arno was leaving me. Why did our love have to be so brief? I tried to tell myself that all was not yet lost. Our S transport was due to leave four days later, so there was no time for lamentation. We were leaving home and had to get everything ready. But what should we bring with us? Clothes? Food? Cigarettes? We packed a bit of everything in our cases. Finally, we tidied up the house, leaving everything as if we were going on a summer holiday and wanted things to be in order when we returned. I sat down at the piano for the last time and played two pieces that seemed to convey a sense of hope: Dvořák's waltz in D flat minor and [Christian] Sinding's *Rustle of the Spring*. I then stroked the keys goodbye and closed the lid.

Tuesday, 20 January 1942, was a beautiful winter day with a cloudless sky. We loaded our cases onto a two-wheeled cart and headed for the railway station. My brother and I pulled the cart while my mother and sister walked behind. People who met us either looked away or slipped into doorways to hide their true thoughts. When we reached the train, we could see a huge crowd milling around it: young, old, mothers with children. The crowd was surrounded by uniformed SS men, some of them with dogs on leashes. They were shouting orders and pushing people in. *Alle einsteigen!* 'Everyone get in!' Everything was in confusion. Children were screaming, and mothers were trying to comfort them though they were scared themselves. Father's words rang in my ears: 'Just keep calm. Remember, calmness is strength.' I wondered where he was now.

Before the train left, every compartment was locked and brown-uniformed *Schutzpolizei*—police guards—were ordered to keep watch over us. They carried short whips and patrolled the whole train. When they came into a coach, they cried *Achtung!* And everyone had to get up and stand to attention. If you did not, or if you were asleep, you were whipped across the face.

It took two days and two nights for us to reach our destination, Terezín. Although it was surrounded by walls, we comforted ourselves that we were still on the territory of our Czechoslovak Republic. The gendarmes were speaking Czech, which seemed a good sign. The dominant feature of the town was a group of about ten barracks, three or four stories high. Our family was now split up—my brother went off with the other men to one barracks while we three women moved into another. We were lucky to have a bunk by the window. We were instructed to elect a *Zimmerälteste* or 'room leader', whose most important task was to divide up the bread ration twice a week. We had to accustom ourselves very quickly to living in one room with many other people. We were all in the same situation, but everybody reacted differently.

I was concerned about where to meet Arno. I had found out that he was in a building around the corner, but he seemed as far away as if he were living on another planet. After one week I started to get really worried. Perhaps they would send him to the East? One day the rumour spread that a new supply of potatoes had reached the barracks. Suddenly I could hear our signature tune being whistled, loud and clear. It had to be Arno! I ran over to the gallery so fast that I almost toppled down into the courtyard from the third floor. There he was, standing with six other men next to a cartload of potatoes.

I ran down the staircase, and our eyes met immediately. We were frantically longing to fall into each other's arms. But where? Somehow we managed to get away from the others and ran down the stairs to the cellar of one of the barracks. There were storage rooms with iron doors. The first two were locked, but the third opened and gave way when we pushed at it. In a dark corner by the door we kissed with insane passion—and all the rest. There was nothing but us and this moment. Suddenly we heard footsteps in the corridor outside, and then we heard the voices of SS men. This was an extremely dangerous situation—we would probably be shot if they found us.

One of the SS soldiers evidently wondered why one door was not locked like the others. He pushed it open, and it banged against the wall, creating a little corner where we stood close together. I could see the soles of his boots. The SS men switched on powerful torches, and for what seemed like an eternity the cone of brightness travelled over the walls and the floor. Then suddenly the commanding officer shouted: *Weiter gehen!* 'Move on!' They left the room we were in, banging the door behind them. What would happen to us if they locked us in? But they did not. As soon as their footsteps had died away, we ran upstairs into the courtyard. I resumed my place among the potato peelers while Arno joined his own squad. We exchanged a quick look of farewell.

As people arrived in Terezín, and when they left it again, every name had to be recorded along with the person's age and transport number. If you were unlucky, you got a pink slip with your name and transport number on it. Then you had to present yourself within 24 hours at the train standing on the siding. There you were forced into a cattle truck which the Germans locked, and then the train drove off into the unknown with its human cargo.

This was the fate of Arno and his family, one day in June 1942. When he came to tell me, all he could say was, 'We have been put on a penal transport. It is a reprisal for the killing of Heydrich.' We all knew that the German official in Prague, *Reichsprotektor* Reinhard Heydrich, had been assassinated.

I was dumbstruck. His transport of 2,000 people was to leave the following day. At four o'clock that morning Arno was standing over my bunk. I have no idea how he got into our barracks at that time of night. He took my hand, slipped a little tin ring over my finger and said, 'That's for our engagement. And to keep you safe. If we're both alive when the war ends, I'll find you.' He embraced me and kissed me, and jumped down. Then he was gone. At five o'clock he left with his transport. On the inside of his homemade ring he had engraved *Arno 13.6.1942.*

Arno's departure left me devastated. He and his entire transport had vanished, there were not even rumours as to where they might have been taken. What was the difference between an everyday transport 'to the East' and a 'penal transport'? We did not know the answer.

Life in Terezín went on, and gradually our hope of being allowed to return home dwindled. In 1943 there were fewer transports to the East, and a period of apparent calm spread through the camp. Amongst the people who came in during this period were many artists—musicians, composers, actors, directors—who had been part of the cultural life of Prague before the war. So the question was: could we do something here? What would the Germans say? As it turned out, the Germans said, 'Why not?' Of course, they had a reason. They wanted a peaceful atmosphere in the town, not a revolt. And they knew we were sentenced to death. The smiles would soon be wiped off our faces. So they said yes, you can perform whatever you like, and we will call it *Freundschafsabende*— 'Evenings of friendship'. You know, this was like a green light for all the artists. Immediately, they went to work.

On top of the military barracks there were huge attics. They were adapted for theatre. There were people that sorted everything from building a stage and wooden benches to costumes and so on. Immediately there were active theatre groups, with professional actors and directors. One group put on a play by [Nikolaj] Gogol, *The Marriage*. The other two were cabarets – political cabarets created on the spot. There was also a German theatre with Kurt Gerron. Gerron was the famous actor who acted with Marlene Dietrich in *The Blue Angel* and who had performed 'Mack the Knife' in [Bertolt] Brecht's musical *Die Dreigroschenoper* (*The Threepenny Opera*).

And then there were the compositions. Unfortunately, most of them were lost. But some have been recovered. I was in Prague earlier this year [2013] and listened to the works of five [of those] composers. So they left something behind. There was a musical genius named Viktor Ullmann, who was a pupil of [Arnold] Schönberg. He composed music for piano and for opera. The opera was called *Der Kaiser von Atlantis (The Emperor of Atlantis)*. A young poet, Peter Kien, wrote the libretto, and the opera was brought to dress rehearsal. The story of *The Emperor of Atlantis* was as follows: there was a mad emperor who waged war with everybody and everywhere. People were dying all over the place, and there were so many dead that Death gave notice—went on strike, and people could not die. The emperor called Death in for an audience and said, 'We cannot go on like this. People have to die. You have to go back to work. Are you willing to do that?' And Death said, 'Yes, on one condition: you will be the first one to die.'

As the opening Ullmann had chosen to play the German national anthem, backwards. When the Jewish management who were invited to the rehearsal discovered this, they got frightened. They were afraid of what the Germans would do when they understood that the Emperor was Hitler, and so on. So the play was cancelled, and the opera was never played in Terezín. But the music was salvaged, hidden under bricks, and thirty years later the first production took place in Holland. Then it was produced in England, and now in America. We later learnt that Gerron, Ullmann and Kien all died in Auschwitz.

People like these were the creative force of art. There is a lady who lives in London, Alice Herz-Sommer. She is a pianist. She gave about one hundred concerts in Terezín, and she survived because she never left the camp. She is 109 years old now (summer 2013). I visited her the other day. She plays the piano every day. Ullmann composed three sonatas for her.

Cultural life in Terezín was unique. It was not commercial, it was not entertainment; it was moral support. I took part in the theatre performances: over two and a half years I was in six plays. In that way, for me, Terezín was a paradise. I worked together with people I would never have had the chance to meet, let alone work with, in my home town. For me, who was so young, that was wonderful. What came after, is another story.

Miraculously, my family, except for Father, managed to hold together. But one day Grandmother was put on a transport list. Sick as she was, she had to go East. It was a cruel leave-taking. I was missing Arno badly. He had been gone for nearly two years. Where might he be? Was he in a camp? People mentioned words like 'Auschwitz' and 'Birkenau'.

In the spring of 1944 a delegation from the International Red Cross came to visit Terezín and see for themselves the 'paradise' that Hitler himself had designed for the Jews. To make the camp appear less crowded, 7,000 inmates were sent to the East. Everything was done to make the streets and squares that the members of the international commission would be passing through appear as pretty as possible, and to make the inmates seem happy and content. For example, a group of pretty girls, including my sister Lydia, were ordered to cross the square carrying rakes over their shoulders and strolling to a tune, as if finishing a day's gardening. Karel Ančerl conducted his orchestra in the concert hall, and a choir directed by Raphael Schächter sang Verdi's *Requiem*. The international commission left, entirely convinced of the authenticity of the Terezín paradise. Immediately after the inspection several transports left for the East.

In the autumn of 1944 the population of Terezín was thinning out visibly. On 15 October we were summoned to join the eastward transport. My brother had been sent off the week before. What remained of my family—Mother, my sister and me—tried to prepare for the journey as best we could. The Germans themselves organized the transports using cattle trucks. We were counted over and over again. Then, in the early morning of 17 October, we climbed into the trucks and the train moved off. Where to? We had no idea. Only fear and uncertainty remained.

There were over one hundred people in our truck, including little children who were thirsty and kept crying. The trucks were bolted from the outside. There were no windows, and the air was hard to breathe, and there were only two buckets for sanitation. Some people prayed, some had given up hope. Three died before we had reached our destination.

Suddenly, after 29 hours in that train, we saw a station sign: AUSCHWITZ-BIRKENAU. The train came to a halt. As soon as the doors were opened, noise and confusion broke out. There were uniformed guards holding dogs on their leashes, shouting *Raus! Raus!* 'Out! Out!' There was no platform where the train had stopped. I took a deep breath, and the air smelled of smoke, with a curious, sweetish tang. There must be a slaughterhouse nearby, I thought, where they are burning the parts of animals they cannot use. No other explanation occurred to me.

I arrived in Auschwitz as a normal person, because I did not take the surroundings as having anything to do with me. Yet the vision of what I saw was so colossal that I had to ask: where am I? What is this? No one had prepared me for such a scene. Blocks of barracks without windows, high fences of electrified barbed wire, dogs, guards. It felt like falling into a deep cellar, where there is darkness and no way out. That was the feeling—that I was caught in an unknown, terrifying underworld.

Suddenly, and quite unexpectedly, I heard a voice. It was not like a human voice you hear, but more like a laser. And the voice, wherever it came from, said, 'This place means death. If you are lucky and they don't kill you, you have enough strength to survive. But it will not be easy.' When I heard this voice, whatever it was, I felt very happy. I felt as though part of a larger something. That there was a guiding hand over me, showing me the way.

In Auschwitz, normal logic did not work. Let me give you one example. As our transport of one thousand people arrived, we first had to march for more than a kilometer. Finally, the column of people arrived at a place where three SS officers, in perfect uniforms, were standing with legs astride. The one in the middle was wearing gloves, and he was dividing the column very quickly—*Links! Links! Rechts! Links! Links! Rechts!*—like a traffic policeman. There was no time to even think. What we did not know, was that left meant instant death, and right, still a chance. I could see that to the left went old people and women with children, while young people went to the right.

Now it was our turn. I looked the officer in the face. He was a handsome man, not evil-looking, though his clear blue eyes had a glint of cold steel. *Links!* he said to my mother. And then *Rechts!* to me. To my sister Lydia he said nothing. In a flash I grabbed her arm and pulled her to the right, next to me. I just had time to catch Mother's terrified look. And then she was gone.

Lydia and I found ourselves in a group of some 300 healthy young women. As we were taken by a women guard across some yard, I could see a group of naked women with no hair, running in a groove. You are still normal, you think, 'Who are these people? What are they doing?' Little did we know that 24 hours later it would be us.

We were put into a wooden barracks and were ordered to take off all our clothes. Jewellery, rings and watches were to be left with our clothes. I took everything off except the ring that Arno had given me. For that ring was my source of strength, my hope of reunion, and my torch of love. We then had to go through a narrow opening in a single file to be further inspected by a uniformed SS man who made sure that we were not trying to hide or smuggle something. It was almost my turn when we heard cries, blows and confusion. It turned out that one of the girls had tried to conceal an engagement ring under her tongue and the SS man had found it. She was beaten and taken away.

The girl in front of me noticed that I still had my ring on. 'For Christ's sake, take that ring off! You must be mad! He'll kill you! And just for a piece of tin!' I started moving backwards in the queue to give myself time to think. If I throw it away, I thought, I will have deserted Arno in my own eyes and lost the moral ground under my feet. If I keep it, the SS man may find it, or he may not. It was like Russian roulette. Putting my life on the line, I also put the ring under my tongue and stepped in front of the SS man. He started ruffling through my hair to see what he could find. At that moment, an order came from his superior to speed up the inspection. 'Next one! Hurry up!' The ring stayed with me. The fact that I had saved the ring gave me fresh confidence that I had nothing to be afraid of.

Each of us then had to go to a 'barber': about ten male guards with clippers in their hands, who had to shave all our hair from our bodies. We were changed beyond recognition. Later, a guard threw at us pieces of clothing from different piles. I found myself holding an olive-green evening gown with pearls. Who, I wondered, could have been the owner of the green dress I was now wearing? Why did she bring it here? What sort of place did she imagine she was going to? The dress had a nineteenth-century look and might have been worn in a stage play about society ladies who dressed for dinner. Now I would have to wear it in a different sort of play, with a different setting and plot.

Finally, we reached the quarters assigned to us, a long and windowless shack with three tiers of bunks. I fell asleep with the others on the hard wooden planks. At five in the morning we could hear the voice of the SS woman in command: *Alle heraus! Zählappell! Raus!* 'All out! Roll call! Out! Out!' We jumped down, half asleep, and made our way out onto a huge parade ground. It was still dark. The counting began: 5, 10, 15, 20 ... and so on. We were counted over and over again, and in between the counting we just had to keep standing there.

Later we were given some soup. This was the first food we had tasted since leaving Terezín. It seemed like ten years ago rather than three days. Terezín had disappeared from our consciousness as if it had never existed. A little later three male prisoners came into our shack; they were working in the camp as electricians and could move about freely. I recognized one of them from Terezín, Ota Weil. I jumped down to greet him. He asked me when I arrived and who was with me, and I told him. He asked, 'Your mother is still with you, or did she go to the left?' 'Yes, she went to the left. So I suppose she is in another block with older women.' Ota took me to the door, opened it halfway and pointed to the column of red flames rising up from a tall chimney. 'That is where she went,' he said dryly. 'She went up the chimney.'

I did not understand what he was saying. I thought, poor Ota, he has been in Auschwitz two years, and all the things he has seen here must have driven him crazy. I felt sorry for him and to avoid further argument I said, 'Yes, I suppose so.' I was still in possession of my senses, while he, poor chap, was not anymore. 'Everyone who went to the left was sent straight up the chimney,' he added, and we said goodbye.

Time was passing, each day like the others. We were either lying on our bunks or standing outside. Hour after hour we stood in order to be counted, over and over again. Then, one night a black lorry stopped in front of our block. Female guards and male guards forced us with whips and truncheons into the lorry, and then bolted it. We had no idea where they were taking us. Finally, the lorry stopped, and immediately the word went round that we were standing in front of a gas chamber.

We were told to get out and stand there until our turn came. The gas chamber was in use, and we had to wait until it was empty. There we stood the whole night and the whole of the following day, with no food or water. I summoned all my strength to stay on my feet and avoid collapsing from thirst and fatigue.

Suddenly, the order came that a transport of 2,000 women, including those of us waiting for the gas chamber, was to be organized immediately and sent further east to dig trenches. In defense against whom? Were the Russians getting closer? Our bare hands against the Russian colossus? Strange turns of fate occurred when least expected. Instead of being consigned to the gas chamber we were now marched off to the railway track. It seemed like a miracle that we should be leaving the horrors of Auschwitz, but the SS guards sneered: *Ihr kommt bald alle sowieso zurück*. 'You will all be back again soon.'

We had no idea where we were going, but after two days and two nights the train stopped, and we got out. We discovered that we were in Upper Silesia, at a place called Kurzbach, not far from Breslau. It was already November. A sharp breeze blew up, it started to drizzle, and we were soon shivering with cold. We were put into a barn with the familiar three-tier bunks, but were given neither food nor drink. Worn out, we simply fell asleep on the cold planks.

There was frost on the ground when the guards woke us up at five, and we were given nothing to eat. They took us to the area where we were supposed to dig trenches. But the soil was frozen so hard that you could not drive a fork into it. So we just stood there for eight hours, freezing in the relentless wind. We were practically barefoot, close-shaven and wearing thin rags. The unequal struggle against the cold drained our willpower and our energy.

Later, in December, as the countryside lay under deep snow and digging became even more difficult, we were ordered to carry logs to a sawmill. This was work for horses, not for starved girls whose health and strength were running out. We were covering 12 kilometers a day. Every evening we applied snow to our sores, but they were still weeping when we got up. Each day one or more of us collapsed with a high temperature and was sent to the 'sick bay', a dark hole where nobody looked after you. There were no drugs or medicine.

Time moved on. It was now early January 1945, and there was still no change on the horizon. Then one day, after we had been counted several times over at evening parade, the *Lagerkommandant* appeared before us with official orders: 'Kurzbach has to be evacuated. Those in the sick bay will stay behind; the rest of you will line up here and march off this evening.'

We set off, marching in fives through the frosty night. We were accompanied by uniformed German guards with rifles. Suddenly we heard violent shouts and screams from the women still in the sick bay, followed by rifle shots.

They had shot every single patient. A deadly silence spread through the countryside.

The Russian army was advancing rapidly westward. The Germans were determined that we, as their prisoners and witnesses to Nazi atrocities, should not fall into Russian hands at any cost. So they were forcing us back west, deep into German territory. We were close to the front and could hear gunfire and explosions day and night. It was music to our ears, for we were confident the Russians would move faster than us and would soon catch up with us.

We had to keep marching on. Day and night, night and day. We were overtaken on the road by lorries crammed with people as the villages in the area were evacuated. The roads were covered with vans and wagons. Lack of sleep was a far worse problem than lack of food. We were at the point of collapse after three days and nights of continuous movement, and the freezing cold made it difficult to breathe.

Our despair produced an idea that saved us. We discovered it was possible to sleep on the march. Whoever's turn it was to take a nap would move to the middle of our fivesome, so that those on each side could take her arms and steer her. Supported in this way, the one in the middle could nod off while her legs were moving automatically. She could sleep for at least two hours like this and get over the deadly exhaustion for a while.

Yet our ranks were starting to thin out. The weaker ones could not keep pace and gradually fell back, which was fatal. Anyone who got out of line and fell in the snow by the wayside was shot without mercy by the nearest German.

I was still together with my sister Lydia. Confirming my worst fears, she now began to fail too. She had been dragging herself along like a ghost. Hanging on to my shoulder she whispered, 'I can't go on any more. Leave me here. You go on.' But somewhere within each of us there is a survival kit. I talked tough to Lydia, and virtually ordered her to march on. She managed to pull herself together. We put her into the centre of our fivesome so that she could sleep a little while we kept walking.

Wherever we stopped, we came to realize that the best place to sleep was with the cattle. There was always a fight for places in the cowshed. It was luxury to lie there on dirty straw with the smell of milk and animal warmth all around. Spending a night with animals, I found out, was not the worst thing in the world. It was less risky, in fact, than with people.

Our numbers were diminishing. More and more girls ended up in the snowdrifts, their corpses lining the route we had taken. It must have been the tenth day of the march when we got to the river Oder in late January. It was flowing fast, with high waves and ice-floes in between. As our column came to a halt, the *Lagerkommandant* suddenly appeared and gave the mystifying command *Wer kann—weiter; wer nicht kann—bleiben*. We turned the words of this Delphi oracle around in every direction and finally decided that it meant 'Whoever has the strength should keep going. Whoever hasn't, stays put.' But he never explained what *weiter* meant. Where to? For how much longer? And what then? And what did *bleiben* mean? The Russians would arrive very soon. Would the Germans hand us over to them alive, or shoot all of us first as they had shot the stragglers on the march?

I had the strength to carry on, and I dragged Lydia with me. There was no bridge or ferry across the river, only open rafts. They loaded as many of us on as the rafts would take without sinking. There was nothing to hold on to, and with the strong current the rafts pushed us violently from side to side. After tossing crazily between waves and ice floes, we finally reached dry ground on the other side. We discovered that only about half of us had survived the journey from Kurzbach.

We marched on for another four days and felt as if we had crossed half the European continent in the last two weeks. I later found out that we had covered nearly 450 kilometers, in rags and virtually without shoes. Finally, we arrived at the gate of Gross Rosen concentration camp. We were glad to have arrived anywhere at all: it hardly mattered that we were behind barbed wire again.

Gross Rosen was mainly a camp for men. Columns of prisoners went past us every day on their way to the mines. But they were hardly human. In their striped coats and convict caps they looked like shadows of men. Their expressionless eyes gazed at us absentmindedly, as if they no longer belonged to this world.

Alive—but dead. Dead—but alive.

Night fell over our new camp. Everything sank into a deep silence. I could not sleep and sneaked out of the hut we were in, surrounded by barbed wire and the silent, clear, frosty night. There was no one around, only the stars winking down at the human race. No, not winking. Rather, they seemed to be observing how trivial and ridiculous man is, with his wars and pride in his silly little victories.

We had been at Gross Rosen just about a week when we heard that Russian units were nearing the camp and that it had to be evacuated. This time a train was awaiting us. We were delighted that we did not have to go on foot, even though it was a goods train with low, open coal trucks. We arrived at the siding where the train stood. The guards ordered us to climb up quickly and stand in the trucks. We were about ninety squeezed side by side in each truck. We thought there was no more room for a mouse, let alone a human being. How wrong we were.

Another group of women waiting on the station platform were now told to join us. Another forty bodies were jammed into each truck. The train moved off, and hysterical cries for help came from those trapped in the centre. At one point of the journey I lost my balance when the others pushed me. Unable to get back on my feet, I spent the night sitting on somebody's corpse. The only place where I could put my hand to prop myself up was on the teeth of the corpse's mouth.

After five days of this hellish journey we came to a halt on a siding. A sign read WEIMAR. Station staff opened the sides of the open trucks. Within a few minutes there were piles of corpses in front of each truck, tossed out like useless human rubbish. And this was Goethe's Weimar, once the symbol of German culture and a high point of civilization. And what about those of us remaining in the trucks? We were happy to have more room.

But our journey was not over. We were to be transferred to a train bound for Buchenwald. But then the Germans discovered that Buchenwald was full. So we were to be taken to a place we had never heard of: Mauthausen. We were half-dead and quite indifferent to where we were going next. The journey went on endlessly, and we believed it would never stop. But then, one cold evening in mid-February, the train stopped at a little hillside station bearing the sign MAUTHAUSEN.

We did not even know which part of Europe we were in. Someone thought it was Austria. Why the Germans at this juncture should be pushing us around from one place to another, sometimes by train, sometimes on foot, nobody could explain to us. All we could see was that there were fewer of us each day.

Mauthausen was a kind of fortress on a hill, and we had to climb up the hill from the station. It was a men's camp, and we were the first female transport to be sent there. In addition to many Jews, the inmates were mostly political prisoners. Around the fortress were granite quarries where the prisoners had to work. Thousands of them perished.

But for us there was no work at Mauthausen. It was evidently just a place for us to stay. Rations consisted once more of a tin of soup a day and a piece of grey bread. Twice a day we were counted at roll-call; the rest of the time we were locked up in our building. After about a week we heard that we going to be sent on somewhere else yet again. We felt like eternal pilgrims. We were frightened by these rumours: judging by our last journey, we were not going to survive this one.

Shortly afterwards we were lined up and marched downhill from the fortress to the station where we had arrived. There was a train waiting for us. Surprisingly, this was neither a cattle train nor a coal train, but a passenger train with coaches marked FIRST class and SECOND class. We thought this was some mistake, but it really *was* our train. Although our destination was unspecified, as always, as we left the station we felt that, this time, things would be better.

For some time we travelled through unknown territory, and we were unsure of our direction. But then we started seeing signs and station names that told us beyond doubt that we were in German-occupied Czechoslovakia. 'Girls, we're back home!' we shouted, and those of us in the coach who were Czech started singing the national anthem, *Kde Domov Muj?* 'Where is my home?' Pulling open the windows, we shouted to people on the roads and station platforms that we were Czech. But nobody reacted. We must have looked like scarecrows.

By strange coincidence, the train slowed down and halted at the station where I and my family had left for Terezín three years earlier. It looked exactly the same. I felt like saying to Lydia, 'Why don't we simply get out and walk straight home?' Just then it seemed possible. But at that point the train jerked, and the journey continued.

At midday on the fifth day the train came to a halt for good. The rails went no further. Once out of the train we could hardly recognize each other. With sunken cheeks and weary eyes, we had the fatalistic look of people who have lost all hope. It was a wintry day in late February. The sun shone but gave little warmth, and there was a layer of snow everywhere. A sign beside the track read BELSEN, with an arrow pointing left. I had yet to learn that Belsen would prove to be the worst of all the concentration camps I was in.

Bergen-Belsen was already crowded with many thousands of prisoners from the camps that had been abandoned further east. Some had arrived by train; some had had to march. Only the toughest had made it. We were put into a block with the same three-tier bunks that we were used to. The daily routine was the same. We got up at five, stood at roll-call to be counted, and were then marched off for 'work', though there was no work to do. The SS women simply led us in formation out into the fields, and there we stood all day, returning to the camp in the evening. We were starving, and I feared for Lydia.

One day on our way back to camp, I spotted something shining in the mud. I picked it up and saw that it was a heavy silver dinner knife. The broadest part of the handle was engraved with a swastika. It must have belonged to the SS officers' mess. They ate off silver. The knife proved very useful. For example, I found different things in the bins outside the SS mess that I could slice with the knife and eat. The knife and Arno's tin ring kept me going.

But then one day as we came back to camp we had an unscheduled body check conducted by Irma Grese, the blonde commander of the women's section of the camp and the most sadistic of our guards. She immediately found the knife on me, pulled it out of my sock and started screaming: *Du jüdischer Dieb! Du elendes Schwein!* 'You Jewish thief! You dirty pig!' Hitting me with the handle as hard as she could, she kicked me and threw the knife furiously into the mud. But I knew I was not going to leave the knife behind. In the confusion around me I crawled back, stretched an arm into the mud—and the knife was mine. Grese did not see me, and I had what I wanted.

Then a typhus epidemic arrived, and all of us fell ill. Lydia was separated from me, and I went staggering from block to block to look for her. Finally, I found my sister. She was lying in a corner on a board, half-dead. Her eyes lit up faintly when she saw me. She held my hand, beseeching me not to leave her there alone. But I had to go back to my own block. When I came back as early as I could the next day, Lydia was no longer there. The board she had been lying on was empty. She was seventeen.

When the British Army liberated Bergen-Belsen on 15 April 1945, they found 20,000 corpses, either in heaps or scattered around the camp. These were not normal corpses but bones covered with skin. The Germans fled, but some of them were captured. The British were shocked: they had come across a real hell which they did not imagine existed. What the British first did was to bring in bulldozers to push the corpses into an open grave. The others were still inside the barracks. I was lying on the floor of one of them together with 300 others who also had typhus. We were just waiting to die.

I believe we have a kind of computer inside of us, and this computer has the ability to eliminate physical functions which it does not regard as important for survival. And in the end it eliminates all emotions. So at the end of the war, in Bergen-Belsen, there was no laughter, no despair, no sadness, no feelings, no hope. It was all wiped out. All you feel is that you are still breathing and that your heart is still beating. That is all you know, and this is a natural process.

The last day of my life there, I heard the same voice coming to me that I had heard in Auschwitz. It said very clearly: 'This is your end. You cannot go on any further.' And I listened to this voice. But it was not me listening, it was something else, and the answer coming from me was: 'No, not yet.' After this message the most miraculous thing happened, which nobody can explain to me. It was some kind of decision that I was not going to die. Not yet, no. I was lying there on the floor and could not even move my legs. Something was telling me to get out of there. And suddenly I felt that I could move, get on my knees. And I know it was not my energy. Where it came from, that is the mystery.

I got on my knees and crawled between the skeletons, out of the block. I was not thinking, but I remember it was evening, with stars. I was just crawling among the corpses, and suddenly I saw a little light. I crawled towards it. It was a Red Cross station. It did not mean anything to me. The station had a double door; I climbed in and sat behind the closed door. I felt safe and completely happy—as though I were thinking, here I am, nothing can happen to me.

In the middle of the night the door opened, the light came on, and there was an officer in a British uniform. When he saw me, he immediately addressed me in a strict voice—you know, the army has rules, and I should not have been there—and he said, 'What are you doing here?' And I answered in my best English, as though it was my mother tongue, 'I am not doing anything. I am just sitting here.' That was perfectly true. And he said, 'I am sorry, but you cannot stay here. You have to go back to your block, because we are evacuating this camp to the next town called Bergen. When your turn comes, you will be evacuated. I am afraid you can't stay here.' And I looked at him, and in my best English I said, 'I understand what you are saying—you have your rules. But I am afraid I cannot go back. For if I go back to the block, tomorrow morning I will be dead. But if you let me be here, I will live, and you will know that you have saved at least one human life. For you have been here for two weeks now, and you can see that here human life has no value whatsoever. But if it is against your instructions and you cannot leave me here, then I will ask you to shoot me. It will be quicker.'

It was like a scene out of a film. He was standing there looking at me. And suddenly the military mask dropped, and there was a human face underneath. And he said, 'Right. You stay here. I will come and pick you up in the morning.' All I said was: 'Do you have water?' He went somewhere and brought water back. And that water was better than the best champagne in the world. It was clear, clean water which I had not seen for months, for years. He closed the door. I sat there, feeling perfectly safe and happy, not knowing that I was a day off my death.

In the morning the door opened. A military ambulance backed in. The English officer came round and opened the door. I could see four stretchers, all of them occupied. And I thought: If he promised to take me away, where is he going to put me? He brought a fifth stretcher, some kind of a harness, and a sheet. I was still wearing the evening dress which I had received in Auschwitz. I had been in this dress for six months. It was cold, with insects all over. He ripped it off, threw it in the corner, put me in the sheet, and bound me with the harness to the fifth stretcher. He put me in between the other stretchers, closed the door, stepped on the accelerator, and off we went. I had my head close to the door. There was a crack in the door of the ambulance, and as we left I could see Belsen retreating into the distance, into the past. As close as I was to death, I felt I was the healthiest person under the sun.

He was my lucky star—that I heard Fred Astaire, in my little Czech town, singing from Hollywood in *Broadway Melody*, and then learnt English so that I could talk to him. After that I was safe. A few months later I was taken to Sweden under the Count [Folke] Bernadotte and the International Red Cross arrangement. We arrived at Norrköping, and they took us to a large, modern hospital where each of us was given clean, white linen, a fresh-smelling pillow and a soft, warm blanket. We felt we had come straight from hell to heaven.

We were given excellent treatment and first-class food, and slowly our physical condition improved. I remember my first tentative steps in the street outside the building. Here we did not have to wear the Star of David, and no one threatened us with arrest. Quite the opposite, people smiled at us. Our hair grew back, and we could recognize ourselves again. Our spirits rose, and we were looking forward to going home.

Then lists of concentration camps survivors began to appear. I read through them eagerly, hoping to spot the names of Arno and my family.

They never appeared. How was I to accept that everyone of those closest to me had perished? Somewhat later statistics established beyond doubt that everyone who was sent 'to the left' at Auschwitz was led straight to the gas chambers. So was my mother. I did not believe my old acquaintance from Terezín when he told me in Auschwitz that mother had gone 'up the chimney'. But he was right.

I also found out that Arno's 'penal transport', which was part of the Germans' revenge for the assassination of Heydrich, had been sent to Poland in June 1942. Everyone was killed on arrival. The tin ring that Arno had slipped on my finger before he left was all that remained of him. One day a friend told me what had become of my brother Jirka. After his arrival in Auschwitz in the autumn of 1944, he was sent to Gliwice to build a rocket munitions factory. When Russians approached Gliwice in January 1945, he tried to flee, but two SS men caught him and shot him. I could establish nothing about my father.

So no one except me had survived. Our family had vanished. Even our home, I found out, was occupied by strangers. I was alone in a foreign country, without friends or any means. My total worldly wealth consisted of Arno's ring and the swastika-engraved knife I had found in the mud in Bergen-Belsen. For three and a half years I had struggled to survive. I had never given in. Now, safe and free at last, I felt I had nothing and no one to live for. I wished I had stayed in Belsen with the others.

After a while I met a Czech girl, Vera. She had been a dancer in Prague, gone through Belsen, and was now also alone. We became friends and felt better immediately. We decided to stay in Sweden for some time and then think what to do next. We first worked at a biscuit factory at Kungälv in southern Sweden, and then I was fortunate to obtain a post as a secretary at the Czechoslovakian Embassy in Stockholm.

One day I received a letter from someone I had never heard of, a Dr J. Lederer of Prague. He had found my name on a list of camp survivors. Dr Lederer wrote that he had been with my father in Auschwitz for several months. They had left Auschwitz in January 1945 when the camp was evacuated, and they had been on a death march together when my father died two weeks later. Dr Lederer described how courageous my father had been, encouraging people around him. He also wrote that Father had often talked about me. It was his dearest wish that I should survive. Dr Lederer invited me to Prague to tell me more about my father, and I wanted to go as soon as possible.

As it happened, one of our embassy staff was driving back to Prague for Christmas and offered me a lift. This was in December 1946, and as we drove through Germany, we could see cities still in ruins. Finally, Prague rose before us in all its beauty, untouched by the war. The following morning I went to Dr Lederer's apartment on Dlouhá Trída in central Prague. I walked up to the third floor. To the left of his front door there was a white doorbell with a copper plate above it: DR J. LEDERER.

Suddenly I decided that I did not want to hear anything more about my father. I did not want to know details about his suffering, or how or where he had died. I could see him standing in the doorway of our home in Rokycany, raising his hat to us and saying, as the Gestapo led him off: 'Just keep calm. Remember, calmness is strength.' That was how I wanted to remember him.

I slowly walked down the stairs and out on to the street. I never met Dr Lederer. Thus I closed the final chapter of our family album and put it deep down into the safe box of my memory. Two days later I returned to Sweden. I did not return to my home again until nearly fifty years later.

So who are we, we people? What is in us? What is our God? Whose energy was it that helped me to climb out of that block in Bergen-Belsen? It was not *my* energy. I concluded that we people have a spirit. Maybe it is different in different people. But my human spirit had the ability to connect to a larger cosmos and harness the energy from there to me. For it was not mine. And so I believe that we are part of the universe, where nothing happens by chance. Rather, things happen when they have to happen, and so does our life.

This brought me to the conclusion that death does not exist. What we call death is a transition from one state to another. And the energy that we have, and what we call spirit, goes on. Only the physical part drops off. It is as though we all have a tiny tape recorder from the moment we are born, where all our experiences are recorded. And when the time comes for division between the body and the soul, the tape recorder goes with the soul. How long we are around, we do not know; we are not supposed to know. But my experience proves to me that we are part of the universe, and we know very little about it. Our existence is part of that big, big programme. I am not afraid of death. I am looking forward to my next existence, though I will not be able to send you a postcard from there. So my life is happy. I have come to terms with my past, and I will say that what I went through has enriched my life. Why? Because I have learnt something that not everybody learns: the values of life. When you are the lowest, closest to your death, what are these values? Not many. Life, human relationships—that is what matters. Material things are important, but not *that* important. We do not need much—we actually need very little. But we need peace of mind, and the ability to live in the moment.

I lived in Australia for twenty years, and there is a link between my

Holocaust experience and what I have learnt from the Aborigines. In their vocabulary they do not have a word for 'yesterday' or for 'tomorrow', only for 'today'. And that is what matters. As when we are sitting here now, together. Yesterday is already gone. Tomorrow is a fantasy. But how many people catch today? Very few. If you just think of yesterday or tomorrow, today goes through your fingers like water, instead of you using it and enjoying it.

I am 91, and I am healthy. In a way your age does not change; it is your attitude that counts. In the end you do not fight with your physical strength but with your mental strength. It is mind over matter. It is the will to survive, which is fed by love and hope. These two things have a tremendous power. We people do not really know what we are made of, or how much strength we have—because in normal life we never need it. But when it comes to a crisis, then you start finding out what you are made of.

And there was a division, which I did not really appreciate until after the war. There were the victims. And if you feel like a victim, you become one. It drains your energy, you are afraid, you worry, you become weaker and weaker. And in the end, when things get really bad, you die.

The other half, a small minority to which I belonged, were the observers. It never occurred to me that what happened around me had anything to do with me personally. It had nothing to do with me at all. I just happened to be there. I could not see any connection between me and what was happening. So I was looking outward. Where am I? What is the barbed wire, the guards, the dogs? I was not afraid, because I did not know what I should be afraid of. And yet I had a feeling that I was strong enough, that I could cope. And the way to do it was to make a little circle around your feet and see this as your territory. You worry about yourself. You accept the situation as it comes, and you adjust to it. That, I found after the war, is the recipe for survival. This is what I was doing until the end. Physically, I would have been described as dead—as being unable to cope. But it never occurred to me that I could die. It just did not enter my mind.

When I look back over that era: Hitler was in power from 1933 to 1945—*sub specie aeternitatis*—that is nothing. And yet, look what happened. It was a reign of the devil for twelve years. It seems to me as though a huge tsunami poured over Europe, leaving an unbelievable human tragedy behind. We, lucky humans, we do not remember pain. We remember dates, events, but fortunately not pain. When I look back, I remember what happened to me during the six war years as though I had died and then came back to life. I have a new life—and I have learnt from the events and the experience. Every day is a gift. Everybody who was sent to a camp came in his or her unique state of mind. So they reacted differently. There were six million murdered.

If they all survived, there would be six million different stories. The Holocaust is not just a historical event. It is a warning.

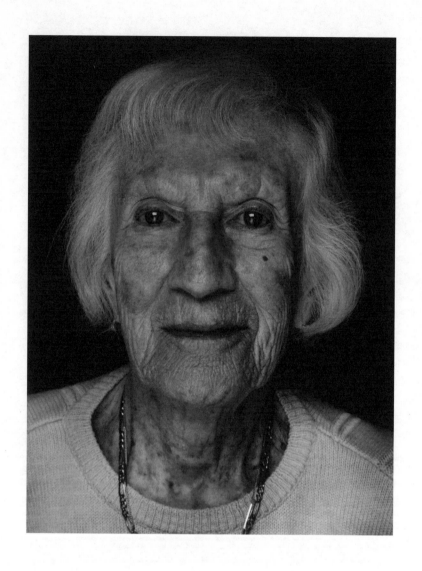

Blanche Major

Born on 3 June 1925. Deported to Auschwitz in spring 1944 and later sent to Buchenwald and Stadtallendorf. Lived in Oslo until her death in 2014.

I was born in the town of Egerag in Hungary. My parents had settled there before World War One. They ran a general store and had a small two-room apartment next door.

When World War One broke out, Father was conscripted to the front. He fought on the German side and was wounded in a brutal charge. A grenade exploded close by the trench he was lying in, and his body was hit by fragments. Incredibly enough, he survived both this charge and the rest of the war. Following the German capitulation in November 1918 he was able to return to Egerag, where Mother had tried to keep the shop running while he was at the front.

In 1922 Mother and Father had a daughter, Ibolya, nicknamed Ibi. Three years later Ibi had a sister, and that was me. The first years of my childhood were a happy time. The Sabbath celebrations were highlights in our little family. It was a holy day, and it was at the same time a reminder that we were a Jewish family. Mother cleaned the house and took the white tablecloth out from the chest of drawers. It was also she who blessed the wax candles.

An episode from 1931 has stuck in my mind. I was six years old and had just started school. The teacher had just ended the Christianity lesson, and it was the death of Jesus on the cross at Calvary which had been the topic of the lesson that day. I do not remember what the teacher said in class, but I remember very well what happened afterwards. No sooner had the pupils entered the schoolyard before they flocked around me. Profanities were hurled about the dreadful Jews, and it all culminated in a friend shouting angrily: 'Blanche—you killed Jesus!'

That sentence remained hanging in the air, and it was as if something inside me was killed in that moment. I had never noticed that my friends did not like me. But it was as if this little sentence encompassed a hatred I did not know about. Even though I was only a little girl, I understood that there was something sinister behind it. And where had they learned about the dreadful Jews? I did not even know who Jesus was, so I ran home as fast as I could, sobbing, and shouted to my mother: 'Who is it that we have killed?' Mother tried to comfort me as best she could, but how could she manage to explain to a small child of six what anti-Semitism was? It was an upsetting and strange evening, and I lay awake for a long time before I could sleep.

When you are regarded as different and as a second-rate citizen, it does something to your innermost self. You get a feeling of being inferior and subservient. It was precisely that feeling I got this painful day, and it would follow me for many years to come. I have always felt different. After that I have thought about the importance of being careful when we talk about other people—especially if there are children present.

Following that incident our family grew more and more isolated. We had always felt safe in Egerag. But now a divide had between created between the other children and the children in our family.

When I had finished school in Egerag, I moved to my grandmother's to go on to middle school. Gran lived in the city of Pécs, which is in south-west Hungary. I liked this town, which was a new world to me. Pécs is an old city which is known for its cultural traditions. Here people of different religions lived peacefully together—Christians, Muslims and Jews. Several of the Jewish families had lived here for many generations. They worked as artisans and tradesmen. They kept to their traditions but were also assimilated and proud of their Hungarian cultural heritage.

Like most youths, my friends and I were also concerned about what was happening around us. I remember that many defended the new German national socialist movement which was led by Adolf Hitler after his rise to power in Germany. But we felt that Pécs was a long way from Berlin, so we tried to put our fears at rest.

As mentioned, I liked it in Pécs; I found new friends and thrived in the school environment. One of my new friends was Gyuri, or György Mermelstein, which was his real name. Gyuri was the son of the local synagogue cantor, and we soon developed a crush on each other. One day we received the painful message that he was going to be sent to the Eastern Front. Hungary had entered into an alliance with Germany, and so Hungary mobilised as well. I was extremely sad when Gyuri was forcibly shipped eastwards in 1942.

Now there was a demand for young men who could be of use in the war—also the Jewish boys were good enough as forced labourers in the Hungarian labour brigade. But at this time these boys were banned from wearing uniforms like the Hungarians did. Instead they were equipped with a uniform cap and a yellow armband. In this way they had been provided with a 'uniform' in such a way that everyone could tell they were Jews. In a short span of time close to 60,000 Hungarian Jews were sent east to the front. None of them knew in advance where they would be forcibly stationed. Nor were they accepted as the other soldiers were, and they were often treated worse by the Hungarian command than by the Germans.

The Hungarian Jews on the Eastern Front suffered enormous losses, and only about 5,000 returned home. Many of the Jewish boys had by then already been sent to the concentration camp Mauthausen, where they were made to do heavy manual labour in the rock quarry. Gyuri survived against all odds and returned after 17 months at the front. He had seen most of his friends be killed—either through executions, starvation, illness or deportation to other camps. When I finally got to meet him again, he barely weighed 40 kilos. The time in the labour camp had made him a shadow of his former self.

In early 1944 Hitler turned against the country that had been his ally. He was of the opinion that Hungary acted more like a neutral state than one of Germany's 'true friends'. On Sunday, 19 March 1944, Nazi Germany occupied an allied nation.

After this the situation for us Jews deteriorated rapidly. Once the first anti-Semitic regulations had been introduced, it was not long before the deportations started. But truthfully, the new regime did not have to work very hard. Quite a few of our fellow countrymen, not least the members of the Arrow Cross Party, were eager to execute the occupants' orders. You can endure a lot from an enemy, but it is considerably worse when the malice originates with your own. And in those days the dark side of the soul of the Hungarian people became ever more evident. Many people now saw the opportunity to make Hungary *Judenrein*, cleansed of Jews.

It was hurtful to discover that people we had believed were our friends betrayed us at the crucial moment. In Egerag the situation grew intolerable for Mother and Father. They no longer had any means to earn a living and had to travel to Pécs to live with family there.

Rumours started to circulate. They said that Jews everywhere were being arrested and sent to different camps and exterminated. We could not believe it—that Germany, which we regarded as the ultimate cultural nation of Europe, could do something like this. That this could happen in broad daylight in a country that had fostered so many composers, authors, philosophers and well-known cultural figures. We could not believe that enlightened people could commit such atrocities. In retrospect, the rumours would turn out to be true.

A scant three weeks later—specifically, on 6 April—Hungary introduced the scheme that meant that all Jews had to wear the Star of David. This decision applied to everyone from six years and upwards. Just like that it became much easier to distinguish us Jews from the rest of the population. The Star of David was like a stamp which justified that everybody could do what they wanted with us. At the same time the yellow star marked us as being different. According to Nazi ideology, we Jews were at the bottom rung of the social ladder. We were designated as Europe's vermin, on par with rats and cockroaches. We became lawful prey for everybody.

One of the peculiar rumours that began to fly around was that unmarried Jewish women would be arrested and sent to German brothels. I was only 19 years old and was very frightened by these rumours. I was terrified this would happen to me, and my boyfriend, Gyuri, was no less scared. In all haste a wedding was arranged for us, and on 4 May 1944 we had a civil wedding ceremony. For a short while we felt safe. But reality soon caught up with us.

Not long after the occupation three of the streets on the outskirts of Pécs were closed off. Military personnel drove in with large rolls of barbed wire. They worked quickly and efficiently, and very soon the streets had been fenced in. Pécs now had its own Jewish ghetto. It was not long before all the Jewish families were visited by the regime's henchmen who, weapons in hand, ordered us to move into the ghetto. Here about 3,000 people would be squeezed into a small area.

I clearly remember the day we were sent into the ghetto. We were only given 30 minutes before we were crammed together on trucks and driven into the ghetto. It was already filled with Jews. We were allowed to pack 25 kilos. But what should you bring? In many places people were lined up along the travel route, and there was no doubt that many felt that the time had now come to get rid of us.

In the ghetto each family was allotted one room, and we were constantly watched by Hungarian gendarmes. We were not worth anything—we were made to feel that as we were chased around. We were like dangerous criminals society had to be protected from. Since we were not allowed to work, our financial situation grew dramatically worse. At the same time the food rations became smaller and smaller. The situation grew worse day by day, but we did not know anything about the occupants' further plans. Fenced in behind barbed wire and with armed guards watching us, there was little or nothing we could do.

We tried to make daily life work as best we could. Those who were teachers tried to instruct the children to the extent that was possible. And the rabbi did his best to preserve the religious practices under very spartan conditions. At night somebody occasionally managed to sneak out to try to get hold of some potatoes or bread to alleviate the starvation in their family.

The situation in the ghetto worsened day by day. The unease was tangible. Could what we had heard really be true: that they sent the Jews to large extermination camps? On 1 June 1944 we received the message that all able-bodied men between the ages of 19 and 45 were to be sent to do forced labour for the Third Reich. Gyuri's name was among those on the list.

We both felt that we also ought to marry in the Jewish tradition. The wedding was held in the ghetto, and the rabbi officiated. It was a beautiful day in early summer, precisely one month after our civil wedding ceremony. Usually the wedding dress has bright colours, and the bride often wears a lot of silver and gold, typically in the form of coins sewn onto ribbons. But I got married in a black dress and white blouse. The only colour that brightened up the ensemble was the compulsory yellow Star of David.

We did not get many days together. Only two days later the SS soldiers marched into the ghetto and collected young Jewish men, Gyuri amongst them. From then on there was no contact between us. I did not know where he had been sent, or if he was still alive. Many rumours circulated, and it was torture living with the uncertainty day after day.

Up until the invasion in 1944 Hungary had been a sanctuary for Jews. When the deportations began in Poland, many Polish Jews fled to Hungary. The stories they told were so gruesome that many of us refused to believe it. It was quite simply too preposterous to be true. We did not understand the consequences of the Nazis' views on human nature and their views on Jews. Probably it was that we did not want to realise the truth, but rather repress it. Deep inside I did not believe that we would be sent out of Hungary either.

But I was wrong—very wrong. Not long afterwards the first transports of Jews from the ghetto started. Nobody knew where they were going, only that we at any time could be told to be ready for departure. The number of people in the ghetto had now risen to over 4,000, and the sanitary conditions had severely deteriorated.

In the final week of June those of us who were left in the camp were suddenly moved into a barracks. This was to have more control over us when the transports took place. We were only allowed to bring essentials to the barracks. There we lived in a stables, seven of us to a box. Nobody had bothered to clean up after the horses, and we simply had to accept lying on straw and horse manure.

We had a feeling that something catastrophic was on the horizon when it became clear that both small children and elderly people would be on the transports as well. After all, they could not work. The situation was difficult, and many developed psychological problems. All the time we were guarded by soldiers with guard dogs and rifles loaded with live ammunition.

On Tuesday, 4 July, a month to the day after our wedding, an SS battalion thundered through the streets of Pécs, turned into the ghetto and fell into formation. Our turn had come to be transported. The officer in charge took his place and ordered us to pack our belongings in a suitcase. We were only allowed to bring the essentials.

I remember clear as day what happened on this momentous day. What were we going to bring? And where were we going? None of us had any idea that we were going to be sent out of the country. I thought we were going to a labour camp and therefore put a pair of blue overalls into the suitcase. That would be handy when I would be working in the new place, I thought.

The mood in the ghetto was rather fractious, and the soldiers did their bit to increase the level of unease. We were ordered to march as one troop down to the city's railway station. I can still picture it clearly—how we were herded forwards, children and adults, scared and unsure of what lay ahead. At the station area we had to give up all our valuables to the soldiers. This was collected in large piles on some tables that had been placed in front of the Gestapo people. They went about the task thoroughly. If they discovered somebody who tried to hide something, they would be given hits and kicks. Several people were beaten senseless.

Together with my family, I was sent on a journey to an unknown destination. Altogether we were 35 members of my family. The youngest was a five-year-old niece, and the oldest were my paternal grandmother of 92 and my maternal grandmother of 82. Everyone was there: my mother and father and my sister as well. But not my husband, Gyuri. Oh, how I missed him and the safety he radiated. But I did not know where he was or if he was still alive.

166

At the station the engine had been readied. 50 carriages were coupled behind the engine. Standing on the platform, we tried to keep the family together and to shield the youngest so that we would not be separated. But everything happened so quickly. Orders were barked in German and Hungarian, and those who did not catch the orders quickly enough were both kicked and beaten. We were forced into baggage carriages, sort of like cattle. They were indeed called 'cattle carriages'. 70–80 frightened persons in each carriage.

I and my sister Ibi ended up in the same carriage as Mother and Father, whereas the other members of the family were in other carriages. The soldiers really knew how to organise things, and before we knew it, the doors closed behind us with a clang. Horrified, we discovered that they could not be opened from the inside. We were, in short, trapped. I felt as if I was going to suffocate because of the crowd and the pressure coming from all directions, and that was before the journey had even started.

With a jolt, the train began to move. We were around 4,000 souls on board—each with his or her own history. All age groups were represented, from newborns to ancients. But we had two things in common: we were all of Jewish heritage, and we were all on our way to our own extermination. But we did not yet know that.

There was nowhere to sit in the carriage; we had to stand upright. Day and night. We did not get any fresh air, nor water. The rain we had when we departed Pécs had gradually been succeeded by a suffocating summer heat. For every kilometre we put behind us, the situation became more precarious. The soldiers had only put two toilet buckets in the carriage. After a few hours they were full, and at each turn the train made the buckets sloshed over so that those who stood closest were soiled. It is as if I can still smell the horrible stench that spread through the carriage.

Nobody cared about our shouts when the train now and then made a stop along the way. The soldiers did not even bother replying, and the doors remained closed. What little we had of water soon disappeared, and several people fainted. In the beginning we could hear the infants crying, and we saw that their faces were flushed from the heat. It was as if they were trying to shout out their protest against the merciless world they were in. After a while the crying turned into weak sobs of exhaustion—and then it was quiet.

Imagine the mothers' despair; there was nothing they could do to relieve their children's suffering. Children and adults died all around us without us being able to do anything to help each other. The dead lay in a heap on the floor. Around me some were praying, while others tried to sing, sort of to keep their spirits up. We tried to keep a conversation going, but it petered out. Those who managed to peer through the cracks in the carriage could report that we passed several towns and urban areas. But no place along the route was familiar to anybody. People were confused. Many became completely apathetic, and the children who were still alive stopped crying.

A lot of what happened during this train ride has been erased from my memory, and good riddance. But I remember that I tried to think positively. I thought that I would certainly need the pair of blue overalls I had brought with me. I would surely be put to work when we arrived, and it was comforting to have my work outfit in order. It was this hope I tried to cling to.

Three days later, in the morning on Friday 7 July, we heard the sound of the train whistle, and we could tell that the carriages were switched onto a different track. Not long after, the train jolted to a stop. For three days and nights we had been standing like sardines in a tin, and our tongues were swollen from thirst. There was an uncanny silence. Now we stood there listening. I cannot remember how long we stood like that, but suddenly the door was wrenched open and yelling soldiers ordered us to jump out. For three days we had been in the dark, so it was a shock when the light hit us.

We were totally unprepared for what met us when the doors were opened. We had arrived at the extermination camp Auschwitz-Birkenau. Outside, there were men with shaved heads, dressed in striped prisoner uniforms. They were to take our luggage and assured us that we would get everything back soon. The platform teemed with armed SS soldiers and Nazi officers who commanded in German: *Los Mensch! Schnell! Schnell!* Trained German shepherd dogs joined the choir; they aided in creating a menacing atmosphere. Those who were not quick enough getting out of the carriages got to taste the rifle butts.

The area was densely dotted with guard towers, all manned by soldiers with machine guns. On both sides of the railway track, behind barbed wire fences, were rows upon rows of barracks as far as the eye could see. Some of the oldest who were already dead remained lying inside the carriage. But afterwards they were thrown out of the carriages and onto trucks. I can—when I close my eyes—picture this over and over, sort of like a film on endless reruns, and hear the creepy sound of their bodies hitting the flatbed.

We were told to put our luggage down and form two lines: men in one line and women in the other. The time had come for sorting and separation. I did not know at the time that the separation was final and that we would never see each other again. Everything happened so quickly that the only one I remember seeing from my family was Mother.

I will never forget her face when she had to leave me. Mother was only 52 years old, but she had been ill a lot, and the strenuous train ride had almost killed her. The last glimpse I had of her was when she walked with the others towards the gas chamber. I do not know what happened to her on this final leg, as there are no eyewitnesses who survived the march that day. There is nobody who can tell me.

I never got to say goodbye to her. Never got to give her a farewell hug. This image has been forever burned into my mind. I have more than once wished that I could erase it. But it is impossible—it is fixed there.

I was not able to say anything to Father or my grandmothers either. Later I was told that they, along with thousands of other Jews, met their deaths in one of the camp's gas chambers. 7 July 1944 became the last day they were alive, and their first and only day in Auschwitz. They were this day's contribution to the chimney smoke and heaps of ashes.

An imposing man caught my attention. He was in a fancy uniform and had a German shepherd by his side. He was clearly in charge, and I thought he would show us some mercy. I could not in my wildest dreams have imagined that this man would over the next quarter of an hour send 33 members of my family to extermination in the gas chamber. When he, with a wave of his hand, sent Mother and Father to the left, I thought they would be taken to a place they could rest after the strenuous journey. How wrong was I.

The impressive man turned out to be Josef Mengele. Both he and others of the Nazi officers were on the lookout for twins among the Jews who had arrived on the train. They had learned the Hungarian word for twins, and they shouted *Ikrek! Ikrek!* when they discovered children who looked alike and were near each other. I know that there were mothers who sent their twins away, hoping that they would be saved. Little did these mothers know that the twins would be used in 'medical experiments' carried out by Dr Mengele and his staff.

As soon as the selection was over, we were herded along by the bellowing soldiers. My sister and I were sent to the right. I remember we passed women and men in striped uniforms. They seemed resigned, and without saying anything, they stared at us new arrivals. At that point I did not have any idea that we would be used as slave labour until the day we were no longer fit for work. At that point it would be our turn to go to the gas chamber. Nor did I understand that the yellow smoke that wafted around us came from the crematoriums where they were burning bodies day and night. Flames erupted from the high chimneys and cast a spooky reddish orange glow over the buildings at night. We could smell the sweetish smell of burned flesh, but still none of us understood what it was.

We no longer had names—now we were only a number. We were sent to the disrobing room where an imperious female SS guard ordered us to undress completely. We had two minutes, and she held a watch in her hand—ready to punish those who could not manage to finish in time. Around us, the soldiers stood with rifles at the ready.

We were allowed to keep our shoes on, and then we were herded into an adjoining room. Somebody came up from behind and grabbed my long hair. I heard the buzz of clippers, and the next moment they had shaved off all the hair on my head and the hair elsewhere on my body. We had no way of protesting. We had been stripped of our own clothes and were now handed a dress. But oddly enough we were allowed to keep our own shoes.

Afterwards, we were divided into groups, and Ibi and I managed to get into the same group. After that we were put in a barracks along with 700 other women. There were no bunks available, so we had to lie directly on the earthen floor of the barracks. We were not given a mattress, nor a blanket. A sign on the wall had the following message: 'One louse—and you are dead.' We would soon understand the meaning of these words. Both the officers and the guards were terrified of catching something from the prisoners, and she who fell ill was in serious trouble.

It was a long night. Thoughts were churning in my head. They went home, to Hungary and to Pécs. Where was my Gyuri? Had he been put in one of these camps too? With thoughts like that I did not get much sleep. All of us new arrivals were almost in a state of shock the first days.

Each morning we were woken up at dawn by the guard who yelled *Aufstehen!* 'Get up!' The next step was to freshen up a little. We tried to wash as best we could, but the conditions were miserable in the dirty and cramped washrooms. The toilet was one single long row of stinking holes. Here we were allotted a few seconds' time to sit, and there was always a long queue.

After that it was time for the count. We could be standing there for several hours, lined up one arm's length from those on either side and the one in front. Around us, officers in uniform lorded over us. Dysentery flourished in the barracks, and some of the prisoners had to use their food bowl as a toilet in the night. The next morning it was a matter of furtively emptying the contents without the guards discovering it.

Whenever we were commanded to do something, it was always meant to be done quickly. We were whipped onward by brutal prison guards. There were many SS women who harassed us and who could do what they wanted with us. Often they proved to be more sadistic than their male colleagues. If anyone was lagging behind, punches would rain down. One human life more or less, young or old, had no value in their system of ideas.

Ibi and I both nourished a strong hope that we one day would be able to return to Hungary. We wanted to go home to tell the world about the violations that were taking place. Most of all, we wanted to be reunited with those of our loved ones who might still be alive. This burning wish was part of the driving force that helped us through the difficult time as prisoners. We *were* going to survive.

Several of our friends were also in the camp. Altogether we were six girl friends who tried to cheer one another up as best we could. Even though we did have some idea about the atrocities that took place around us, we talked little about it. Or about those who had gone to the left. Instead we talked about different food dishes, shared recipes with each other, and planned in detail the dream meal we were going to make as soon as we got back home. We always tried to find something positive in our prison existence. We lived from one hour to the next. We sort of did not dare to hope for anything more than the present day.

Even though the food was terrible, the more experienced prisoners advised us to eat as we would need all the nourishment we could get. We were apparently supposed to be given 200 grams of bread in the morning, and at mid-day something that was supposed to be soup was ladled out. Several days went by before I could manage to eat it. But I quickly found out that there was nothing else to be had, so there was nothing for it but to force the food down.

We were all in a panic over becoming too thin. That meant you were at risk of being picked out in the selections, and that trip went straight to the gas chamber. Such selections were typically held once a month. In block after block the prisoners had to undress and walk naked past a commission of Nazi doctors and officers. They had authority over life and death, and a small note on their pad decided whether we were fit for work or not. No wonder we were terrified when a selection was announced. Alongside the fear of becoming too thin, hunger haunted us all the time. After a while it became a physical and psychological torture that you carried with you through all the twenty-four hours of the day.

On 11 August—five weeks after we had arrived—we noticed frenetic activity in the camp. The camp toilets were a pure rumour mill, and it was repeated over and over that the Third Reich was now beginning to fall apart. At selection that day we were ordered to report for work. A total of 1,000 women were required to work in the German weapons industry. I will never forget the frightened and tense faces that waited to be judged by the Nazi doctors. Who would be picked as being fit for work? We were at the mercy of the doctors' will. How did we look? Had we become so thin and weak that we could no longer be used for work? None of us dared say a single word while the doctors scrutinised us from head to toe and made their notes.

When the inspection was over, all of us six friends had been picked for work. That was a huge relief. We were given orders to shower, and we were handed grey linen dresses—before we were commanded outside for a new assembly. They were paranoid about counting us: the number of prisoners had to tally with the officers' list. This time everything was in order, and the SS people chased us onto trucks. Yet again we were counted, before the tailgates were raised and we started the journey. It lasted three days and nights, with truck and train. We sat close, but not as close as we had done in the cattle carriages. The guards who accompanied us were not SS people but soldiers from the German army. To our surprise we were given water and bread during the transport. This was something new and unexpected, but we did not reflect any further on that, just noted that it was like this.

After three days and nights we were registered in the prison camp Buchenwald and from there sent on to an ammunitions factory in Stadtallendorf, west of Berlin. Stadtallendorf was a forced labour camp, and guards surrounded us everywhere. But they were not as brutal as the SS soldiers we had come to know in Auschwitz. The entire complex was camouflaged by huge embankments which had been planted with trees and bushes so that the Allies would not discover the factory complex and bomb it. It was hard work, with a working day of twelve hours, but the time at the weapons factory undoubtedly saved my life. The work itself, inside the ammunition factory, was both hard and dangerous. We made bombs from poisonous materials, and we did not have any form of protection. The dangerous Tri-poison [trinitrotoluene] which was used in the production made what little hair that had grown out on our heads carrot-coloured, while our fingernails turned brown.

And so I was put to producing weapons that would be used in the German war machine. But at the same time I knew that widespread sabotage was carried out by the slave labourers in the different departments. We frequently 'forgot' to put in vital parts; consequently, the weapons were useless. That was something both I and the others rejoiced at. It was our contribution to stopping the madness of war.

Along with three other women, I had been set to lift 150-kilo bomb crates. It was heavy and far from safe. Our daily food ration was a small piece of ersatz bread and a bowl of soup. The contents can best be described as warm water with a few small vegetable pieces in it—if they had managed to get hold of those, that was. This was what we were meant to survive on, even though the work drained what strength we had left. Here, too, many buckled under.

After a while autumn arrived, and it started to turn cold. Without underwear and stockings, we had to walk four kilometres every morning to get to work.

There was no warmth in the thin linen dresses, but fortunately we were handed thin cardigans which gave a little more warmth. We stuffed rags and paper into our wooden clogs and hoped that would warm us up a little. But little helped against the freezing wind. You can get used to starving, but never to freezing.

Even though the winter was hard, we managed to get through the days somehow. The cold was a trial in the uninsulated barracks. Now and again we wondered whether we would be bombed to death or if we would freeze to death. What really warmed us, was realising that the beginning of the end of the war had started. The behaviour of the SS troops also made us realise this. Something was going to happen. During the assembly on 26 March the soldiers seemed very nervous. While we stood there shivering in the slush, we were told that we were to be evacuated. The seriousness of the situation became clear when we were given the order 'march or get shot'. The labour camp was to be emptied of prisoners, and no witnesses were to remain there alive.

We started marching. Thousands of prisoners of war on a journey. We trudged onwards on roads that in several places had been destroyed in bombing raids by Allied planes. It was cold, close to 20 degrees [Celsius] below zero. We did not have clothes that could withstand that kind of cold, only short dresses and no underwear. Many were without both stockings and shoes, and many could not handle the ordeal this march was. We had not walked many kilometres before the first bodies appeared along the road. Women and men who had buckled under, or who had been shot because they could not manage to walk any further.

After hours of exhausting marching, Ibi and I and several others decided that we would attempt to run away. The opportunity came when we were nearing a dense forest. We managed to slip away at the right moment and ran as fast as we could into the forest without looking back. Luckily, everything was quiet. We looked around in the dark to see if we could discover any lights. Every now and then we heard the roar of canons.

After nearly two days and nights in the forest we suddenly heard the sound of powerful engines approaching. Towards us, through the forest, came military troops and tanks. I cannot describe the joy we felt when we realised they were American soldiers and that they only wished us well. We had been rescued at last. It was difficult for us to understand that we were free, but as we gradually realised this, we began to feel joy. Finally, we could dress in warm clothes, and I remember that we were given chocolate. It tasted delicious. Now we could start to ingest nutritious food. I weighed 35 kilos.

After this, we were in a state of euphoria at actually being alive. None of us talked about what we had gone through. Today, I cannot remember if we asked about our families. It was not that we did not care, we just rejoiced at having survived. It was only much later that I grieved for the dead and that thoughts about what had happened to the other members of my family, and with Gyuri, appeared. At this time we did not know anything about what had happened to the other members of our family after we had been split up on the platform in Auschwitz.

We had nowhere to go, so the Allies arranged shelter for us in the town, Frielenhof. We got new clothes, and I remember that we danced for joy. All of a sudden we were treated like human beings, and we did not have to hear the never-ending *Los, los, Schweinhunde!* from bellowing SS soldiers. Instead we were addressed as 'ladies' by the American soldiers. It was like being gifted life again.

We stayed in Frielenhof until August. But as early as June a Red Cross car came with news from my hometown. Excitedly, we hurried over to the Red Cross representatives and hoped for good news from home. That was when I got the final message, the one I deep inside had tried to steel myself against: 'Blanche—your whole family has been wiped out. All the 33 relatives you travelled alongside were killed in Auschwitz-Birkenau. Only you and Ibi have survived.'

That was a difficult day. Do not ask me how I reacted. I cannot remember even if I want to; it is as if it has been erased. I do not know if I cried. Nor is that relevant. For how do you react to such information? My whole family had been efficiently eradicated by the Nazi killing machinery.

A few days later people arrived in Frielenhof with lists of Jews who had survived the war. I knew that my family was irrevocably gone. I found the names of two of my male cousins and—against all odds—Gyuri's name. I cannot describe what I felt in that moment when I read his name. The anxiety that had been gripping my chest like a claw dissolved, and now I only looked forward to meeting him again. In the final phase of the war he had managed to escape and get to the Swiss embassy in Budapest where he had been granted political asylum.

I went to Hungary as soon as it was possible, and there I found Gyuri. It was strange seeing him again. After all, we had such a short marriage behind us. Like many other Jewish youths we also dreamt of going to Palestine and building a new existence there. We were young, and we owned absolutely nothing.

The war had stolen our youth, and now we discovered that there was no room for us in Hungary either. We were not particularly welcome, and we

174

soon realised that it would not be easy to live on in the country which had collaborated with the Nazis. Still, we were lucky. I remember how proud Gyuri was when he one day told me that he had managed to get a small flat for us in Pécs. For a short while we felt as if we were in paradise. But reality soon caught up with us; it was difficult to find peace in a country where one was not wanted.

We tried to get to Palestine but encountered problems at the border and after a while had to give up on that plan. Then we got the opportunity to go to a refugee camp in Austria. At that time, I had become pregnant and was for that reason suddenly in a completely different situation. Together with my sister, we grasped this opportunity and left Hungary. After a while we were sent from the transit camp to a camp in Windsheim in Germany. This camp was like a waiting camp. It had been established by the Allies and was to provide protection for Jews and others who had become stateless following the Holocaust.

In 1946 I gave birth to Peter in this camp. Now we were a little family of three. But we were still stateless—three persons who nobody wanted. We lived here for a year, together with people from different nations. That year seemed long because everything around us was so uncertain.

Then we received an offer to go to Norway—Ibi as well. It was practically a coincidence that made us leave Germany, heading for Norway. A boat arrived that was going there, and that was when we decided to accept the offer and try to establish a life in Norway. We did not know either the country or the language, but the way the situation was, we did not have much to lose.

We were sent on the troop transport ship *Svalbard*, and at first we were billeted at Ystehede near Halden. There was a shortage of labour after the war, and Gyuri found work at the paper mill in Halden. Here there was also a provisional school, under the leadership of Headmaster Olden.

At first it was Ibi who went to school to learn Norwegian. Gyuri had his job, and I had Peter to look after. After a while Ibi found a job in a tailor's shop in Oslo and moved there. Later, Gyuri, Peter and I also moved to Oslo. In the beginning we lived near Sognsvann, in one of the many barracks built by the Germans during the occupation. Even though the roof leaked and there sometimes were ice puddles on the floor in winter, we were content. We had a place to live and were in the process of building a new life.

We lived in the barracks until 1951, when we moved to a housing area at Oppsal that originally was intended for Jews. We applied for, and were granted, a loan from the Norwegian State Housing Bank. It was a nice time, and we got to know the Norwegians who also lived here very well. Although the houses were popularly known as 'the Jew buildings', we did not notice any form of harassment.

Ibi met Arne Korsmo, and they married in 1951. In 1956 I started a private outdoor child care service with a friend, which we ran for 16 years. Later I worked in the Ministry of Transport and Communications for 20 years, and after a while we could afford a bigger flat. Gyuri worked in the Norwegian branch of Philips [Electronics]. In 1987 he developed heart problems, just as he was retiring. We had some good years together until he died in 2001. It was as if the rug had been pulled out from under me. The years we had shared included tragedy, sorrow and suffering. But we also got to experience starting a new, safe life together and putting the painful traumas at a distance. I am immensely happy for all the good memories I have of Gyuri.

Even though we, by all accounts, had a good life, we carried hidden wounds that the war and the prison camps had dealt us. In Norway we met the doctor and psychiatry professor Leo Eitinger. He had been a prisoner in Auschwitz himself, and he did a great job with helping the refugees. For many years I repressed the memories of Auschwitz and the suffering I lived through in this camp. But in 1980 I was hit by what Eitinger termed KZ syndrome, the concentration camp syndrome. It was as if Auschwitz caught up with me, particularly at night. One detail after the other emerged. I could be back in the cattle carriage, or in the prisoner barracks in Auschwitz.

Towards the end of the 1980s I had become preoccupied with the idea that I had to see Auschwitz again. I talked to Ibi about this, but she could not stand thinking about it. Nor was Gyuri interested in going back. He struggled with bad trauma from the war but never managed to talk about this. He once tried to tell me about some of what he had experienced on the Eastern Front, but it was not much he managed to say before he froze completely and he burst into tears. Instead he carried all the hurt inside.

One day Gyuri came across a small advertisement in *Aftenposten*. Some idealists down in Risør, with a German-born lady as the prime mover, wanted to launch awareness-raising themed tours to the concentration camps. It was the German-born Helga Arntzen who had the idea for 'White Buses to Auschwitz', and I joined her and 70 pupils from Risør lower secondary school on the first trip in August 1992.

It was with a strange feeling that I walked through the gate of Auschwitz-Birkenau again. It was here I lost my family; this place is their graveyard. It was hard, standing there on the selection platform after so many years. While I was standing there, the memories came bubbling forth, and I returned to 7 July 1944. This was where I saw Mother for the last time. At the same time

Father, my uncles and aunts, two grandmothers, and the seven-year-olds Lazi and Agi disappeared.

It was important to me to make this journey. It was also important because I got to tell my story to the young people who had come on the trip. At the same time this trip gave me hope, not least when I saw how the young people reacted to what they saw. Many had read about the camps, but when they went there, they understood.

When the day comes that we who experienced Auschwitz and the Nazis' barbarity are gone, it will be the young people who will have to continue telling this story. The days I got to experience with the young people from Risør have really given me hope for the future.

We held one minute's silence after we had laid down flowers. If we had held one minute's silence for each of the six million Jews who were murdered, we would have been standing there for twelve years.

Why exactly me? Why did I survive? I do not know and cannot give a satisfactory explanation. But I know what is close to my heart: telling new generations and exhorting them to not forget what happened. The worst thing I have experienced after the war are the claims that the gas chambers are lies and Jewish propaganda. We must not become naive. Auschwitz was planned by human beings and built to kill human beings in an industrial genocide. Those of us who survived have a duty to bear witness to the atrocities for as long as we can. As Elie Wiesel said: 'To forget would be the enemy's final triumph.'

We cannot do anything about the past, but I am convinced we can do something about the future.

Textual basis

The narratives in this book have, with one exception, been communicated orally to me. They were recorded on tape and subsequently transcribed and edited. All the time witnesses have read their own text, corrected errors and approved the narrative.

The meetings took place on the following dates: Maria Segal: 15 April 2010 and 11 May 2011; Judith Meisel: 11 May 2011; Edith Notowicz: 11 June 2012 and 17 April 2013; Maria Gabrielsen: 26 June 2012 and 3 April 2013; Blanche Major: 5 November 2012; Isabella Wolf: 29 November 2012 and 25 January 2013; Ella Blumenthal: 12 December 2012 and 19 February 2013; Yvonne Engelman: 13 and 15 March 2012; Olga Horak: 16 March 2012; Zdenka Fantlová: 29 September 2012 and 8 May 2013.

Since Blanche Major had suffered a stroke and partially lost her powers of speech, she was the only one of the time witnesses who was unable to communicate her story orally. With her approval, and with permission from Oddvar Schjølberg, author of *Jeg overlevde Auschwitz. Blanche Major forteller* [I survived Auschwitz. Blanche Major tells her story], I prepared a text in collaboration with Marit Langmyr that I read aloud for Blanche Major. Blanche Major approved this text after a number of adjustments had been made. The revised text was then read, corrected and approved by her son, Peter Major.

The textual basis for the nine other narratives are the interviews referred to above. In a few cases, the oral narratives—in collaboration with the time witnesses and according to their own wishes—have been supplemented by information from books they have written. In all cases, the entire text—including such additional information—has been approved by the time witness. The relevant publications are:

Fantlová, Zdenka. *The Tin Ring*. Newcastle: Northumbria Press, 2010. Now published by McNidder & Grace.

Horak, Olga. *Auschwitz to Australia: A Holocaust Survivor's Memoir*. (Sydney: Jagar Sprinting, 2000). Now distributed by the Sydney Jewish Museum.

Schjølberg, Oddvar. *Angitt av mamma* (Risør: Aktive Fredsforlag, 2006). [About Maria Gabrielsen]

Schjølberg, Oddvar. *Jeg overlevde Auschwitz. Blanche Major forteller* [I survived Auschwitz. Blanche Major tells her story] (Risør: Aktive Fredsforlag, 2009).

Segal, Maria. *Maria's Story: Childhood Memories of the Holocaust* (Santa Barbara: Boehm Group, 2009).

Tak for alt. The Story of Holocaust Survivor and Civil Rights Activist Judith Meisel (1998). Film produced by Laura Bialis and edited by Broderick Fox. DVD approx. 60 mins. Los Angeles: Sirena Films.

Glossary

Aktion Reinhard

Code name for the Nazi plan to murder Polish Jews. Marked the start of the most deadly phase of the Holocaust through the building of extermination camps. See: 'Introduction'.

Aktive Fredsreiser (Travel for Peace)

Norwegian company that arranges awareness-raising school trips, themed tours and documentation tours to, among other destinations, the Nazis' former concentration and extermination camps. http://www.aktive-fredsreiser.no/index.htm

Ančerl, Karel

Czech conductor. In contrast to his wife and young son, he survived both Theresienstadt and Auschwitz.

Anielewicz, Mordecai

Leader of the Jewish Combat Organisation, Żydowska Organizacja Bojowa (ZOB), which rebelled against German forces in the Warsaw ghetto in the spring of 1943. Was killed when the SS conquered his command bunker on 8 May 1943.

Anti-Semitism

Term for antagonistic attitudes and actions directed at Jews because they are Jews.

Arntzen, Helga

Founded Hvite Busser (White Buses to Auschwitz) in 1992 and Aktive Fredsreiser (Travel for Peace) in 1998. Helga Arntzen was born in Germany but has lived in Norway since 1962.

Arrow Cross Party

Pro-German and anti-Semitic political party that ruled Hungary from October 1944 to January 1945.

Astaire, Fred

American actor, dancer and singer.

Auschwitz

See: 'Introduction'.

Barracks leader

See: 'Block', 'Blockälteste'.

Bełżec

Extermination camp in south-east Poland. Between March and December 1942, circa 434,000 Jews and an unknown number of Poles and Roma were deported to this camp, where they were murdered. Very few survived Bełżec.

Benkow, Jo

Former president of the Norwegian Parliament, prominent politician in the Høyre party [Conservative Party], and author of the book Fra synagogen til Løvebakken [From Synagogue to Parliament].

Beriberi

Disorder caused by a deficiency of vitamin B1 which affects the nervous system. Some of the symptoms are lassitude, tremors, joint and muscle pains, and heart palpitations.

Bernadotte, Folke

Swedish count, diplomat and head of the Swedish Red Cross who organised the White Buses that liberated, among others, Norwegian and Danish prisoners from German concentration camps. In 1948 the UN chose Bernadotte as mediator in the Palestine conflict. On 17 September 1948, he was killed by Jewish terrorists in Jerusalem. See also: 'White Buses to Auschwitz'.

Block

Term for a camp barracks.

Blockälteste

German term for the senior barracks inmate or barracks leader; that is, the prisoner who was responsible for maintaining order in a particular barracks. The barracks leader reported to an SS officer who had the overall responsibility for the barracks. See also: '*Funktionshäftling*'.

Brecht, Bertolt

German dramatist and poet.

Buchenwald

This concentration camp near Weimar in Germany was not an extermination camp, but the prisoners were worked hard as forced labourers, and there was a high rate of murder, particularly of Soviet prisoners of war. Of circa 250,000 prisoners during the war, about 56,000 died.

Chełmno

Extermination camp about 50 kilometres northwest of the town Łódź. Over 150,000 people were murdered in Chełmno.

Concentration camp

Heavily guarded prison camp (particularly for civilian dissidents and for ethnic groups) characterised by brutality, insufficient amounts of food and food with little nutritional value, and bad hygienic conditions. Nazi Germany's concentration camps included extermination camps, which particularly focused on the extermination of Jews, and forced labour camps. See also: 'Introduction'.

Czerniaków, Adam

Head of the Jewish council in the Warsaw ghetto. Took his own life in 1942.

Dachau

The first concentration camp in Germany, by the city of Dachau, north of Munich. Construction was begun in the spring of 1933. The camp was a blueprint for later concentration camps. At least 30,000 prisoners died in this camp.

DAW

Abbreviation of Deutsche Ausrüstungswerke, an SS company which produced armaments and which used thousands of prisoners as forced labourers. DAW had factories in both Auschwitz and Sachsenhausen.

Deportation

Forced banishment to a particular place, often far away and unfamiliar to the deportee. Nazi Germany's deportations of Jews and other groups which the regime wanted to exploit and punish, usually were to a concentration camp in Germany or a German-occupied country.

Dietrich, Marlene

German American actress and singer.

Dvořák, Antonín

Czech composer.

Dysentery

Inflammation caused by bacteria. Gives serious diarrhoea which in the worst instance can lead to death.

Einsatzgruppen

Mobile SS units which identified, arrested, and murdered Jews in areas occupied by the German army, particularly on the Eastern Front.

Eitinger, Leo

Czech Jew who arrived in Norway in 1939, 27 years old. He was a prisoner in Auschwitz and Buchenwald and survived along with Samuel Steinmann and Julius Paltiel, who also had been deported from Norway. He became a professor of psychiatry and wrote several works about concentration camp survivors and their physical and mental health. He called late-onset trauma from stays in concentration camps 'KZ syndrome', and won international recognition for that.

Evil

See: 'Introduction'.

Funktionshäftling

A prisoner functionary in the camp's informal organisational hierarchy, such as Kapo, Blockälteste, Lagerälteste, clerks, and Stubenälteste. A barracks leader (Blockälteste) had one or more clerks and Stubenälteste, room leaders, to help with 'running' the barracks. The barracks leaders were under the camp leaders, the Lagerälteste, in the camp hierarchy. The number of functionaries varied from camp to camp according to its size. This unofficial prisoner hierarchy was established to organise and increase the efficiency of the prison camps. That some prisoners were given certain positions in this hierarchy meant that they were in a position where they had power over their fellow prisoners, something which could both have positive and negative effects on camp conditions. Funktionshäftlinge could abuse their power and terrorise their fellow prisoners, or they could use their position to help their fellow inmates as much as they were able. However, this hierarchy of prisoners was under the authority of the SS.

Gerron, Kurt

German Jewish actor and director who was deported to Theresienstadt and later to Auschwitz, where he was murdered.

Gestapo

Abbreviation of Geheime Staatspolizei ('Secret State Police'), the official security police in Germany under National Socialism and in the German-occupied European territories during World War Two.

Ghetto

Segregated area reserved for a group of people. The word comes from the Venetian ghèto ('slag'). Slag from the city's foundries were deposited on the same island where the Jewish ghetto, the first in Europe, was established in 1516 during the Republic of Venice. In this book the word is used to denote Jewish ghettos during World War Two. The Jews were gathered in certain areas of a city which were often overpopulated and nutritional, hygienic, and social disasters. Often the creation of a ghetto simply marked a transitional phase before the Jews were deported onwards to various concentration and extermination camps.

Goethe, Johann Wolfgang von

Germany's most famous writer was a supreme master of all literary genres.

Gogol, Nikolaj

Russian dramatist and author of novels and novellas.

Grese, Irma

Notorious prison guard with the title SS Helferin ('Female SS Helper') and the nickname 'The Beautiful Beast' who worked in the concentration camps Ravensbrück, Auschwitz, and Bergen-Belsen. At the age of 22, she was in the autumn of 1945 sentenced to death by the British military court that tried 48 SS employees at Bergen-Belsen.

Gross-Rosen

The concentration camp Gross-Rosen was established in 1940 as a satellite camp of the concentration camp Sachsenhausen in Lower Silesia in what is today Poland. The camp became an autonomous camp in 1941 and was the head camp of a number of satellite camps, among them Wolfsberg. Wolfsberg belonged to the satellite camp complex Riese in Eulengebirge near Breslau. Of the about 130,000 prisoners at Gross-Rosen, about 40,000 died.

'Go up the chimney'

Concentration camp expression for dying and then being cremated.

Herz-Sommer, Alice

Jewish pianist from Czechoslovakia who gave about 100 concerts in Theresienstadt, survived, and afterwards lived in London. She was born in 1903 and was, until her death in 2014, the world's oldest known Holocaust survivor.

Heydrich, Reinhard

German Nazi politician and SS officer who in 1939 became head of the Reichssicherheitshauptamt (RSHA), the 'Reich Main Security Office', and who played an important role in planning and organising the Holocaust, including as Chair of the Wannsee Conference in January 1942. Heydrich, who was a fighter pilot during the German invasion of Norway in 1940, was killed by the Czech resistance in May 1942. Zdenka Fantlová lives in the building in London where this operation was planned.

Himmler, Heinrich

German Nazi politician, head of the SS with the title Reichsführer SS. Took his own life in May 1945.

Hitler, Adolf

German Nazi politician, Chancellor of Nazi Germany from 1933 to 1945. Took his own life on 10 April 1945.

Hitlerjugend

The Nazi youth organisation for young boys.

HL Center, The

The Center for Studies of the Holocaust and Religious Minorities is located in a house called 'Villa Grande' at Bygdøy in Oslo. This building was called 'Gimle' during the war and was, from 1941 to the German capitulation on 8 May 1945, the private residence of Vidkun Quisling, the leader of the National Socialist Party in Norway and head of the Norwegian puppet government during the war.

Holocaust

The systematic, industrial, government-financed genocide of about six million Jews carried out by Nazi Germany and their allies during World War Two. Closely tied to the Holocaust is the Nazi mass murder of Roma, Poles, Soviet prisoners of war, homosexuals, Jehovah's Witnesses, political prisoners of war, and people with disabilities. The word means 'sacrifice by fire' and comes from an Ancient Greek translation of the Hebrew Bible. The Jews in Eastern Europe used the Yiddish word churb'n ('destruction') or the Hebrew shoah ('disaster'); in Israel the term shoah is still used. See also: 'Introduction'.

Horthy, Miklós

Hungarian admiral and statesman, Hungary's Regent from 1 March 1920 to 15 October 1944.

Höss, Rudolf

Camp commandant of Auschwitz. Was put on trial in Poland in 1947 and sentenced to death.

IG Farben

German chemical manufacturing company which was closely affiliated with Auschwitz through its use of prisoners as forced labourers. Built a factory for the production of synthetic rubber that was connected to the camp and which later became an autonomous camp called Auschwitz-III-Monowitz. This camp had several satellite camps.

Jewish raid of 1942

In October 1942 all Jewish property and all Jewish assets in Norway were seized, and all male Jews arrested. One month later women and children were arrested as well.

Kapo

Abbreviation of Kameradenpolizei ('comrade police'), a prisoner who oversaw a work command and who had one or more work foremen to help him or her supervise the prisoners.

Kien, Peter

Jewish artist and poet, deported to Theresienstadt in December 1941 and in October 1944 to Auschwitz, where he perished along with his wife and his parents.

King, Martin Luther

American Baptist minister, peace activist, and leader of the African American Civil Rights Movement. Awarded the Nobel Peace Prize in 1964.

Kramer, Josef

Camp commandant of Bergen-Belsen. Sentenced to death by a British military court in the autumn of 1945.

Labour camp

See 'Introduction'.

Liszt, Franz

Hungarian piano virtuoso and composer.

Majdanek

See: 'Introduction'.

Masaryk, Jan

Czech politician and Foreign Minister of Czechoslovakia. Son of Tomáš Masaryk.

Masaryk, Tomáš

The first President of Czechoslovakia and a prominent politician in the inter-war period. A champion of a liberal and democratic humanism, he enjoyed an almost legendary popularity.

Mauthausen

The first concentration camp outside the borders of Germany was established near Linz in Austria. Mauthausen was chosen because of the opportunity to quarry granite, and many prisoners were used as forced labourers in the granite quarry. Of circa 200,000 prisoners, about half died. In addition to the many who died because of starvation, execution, beatings, lethal injections or gas. Mauthausen was the only concentration camp which was, along with the extermination camps in the east, designated Lagerstufe III, the worst category of camp.

Mengele, Josef

Human geneticist and SS-Hauptsturmführer who 1943-1945 worked in Birkenau and was in charge of a large number of medical experiments which cost countless prisoners their lives, and of the selections to the gas chambers. He managed to escape to South-America and died in Brazil in 1979 without having been on trial for his crimes.

Mila 18

The headquarters of the Jewish Combat Organisation, Żydowska Organizacja Bojowa (ZOB), which under the leadership of Mordecai Anielewicz rebelled against German forces in the Warsaw ghetto in the spring of 1943.

Muselmänner

Term for prisoners who were severely emaciated to the point that they appeared to be skeletons.

Narrative

See: 'Introduction'.

Natzweiler

The concentration camp Natzweiler-Struthof was established near Strasbourg/ Alsace in 1941, and the prisoners were mostly put to work in the nearby rock quarry. The camp became known as a Nacht-und-Nebel (NN) camp because a large segment of the prisoners belonged to the category NN prisoners, who were to disappear in 'Night and Fog' and who were not allowed to receive parcels or write/receive letters.

Nuremberg Laws

Collective term for two anti-Jewish laws which were introduced during the National Socialist party's Nuremberg Rally in 1935. These laws meant that Jews were stripped of their civil rights and that anti-Semitism was made part of Nazi Germany's official policy.

Oracle of Delphi

The Oracle of Delphi was the oracle of the Greek god Apollo. The prophesies of the oracle priestess, Pythia, were often ambiguous and provoked further interpretation.

Oslo Jewish Museum

Museum which documents and imparts information about Jewish immigration, life, and integration into Norwegian society.

Phlegmon

Pus-producing inflammation of the soft or connective tissues. Because of vitamin and fat deficiencies prisoners often got sores that would not heal.

Pleurisy

Inflammation of the membranes that surround the lungs.

Prisoner categories

The prisoners in German concentration camps were divided into categories, and everybody wore a coloured badge in the shape of a triangle on their prison uniforms. The political prisoners wore red triangles, criminals were marked with green, homosexuals with pink, Jehovah's Witnesses with purple, and the 'asocials' – such as prostitutes, vagrants, beggars, unemployed and some criminals – wore black triangles. Roma were at first marked with brown triangles; later they were often sorted into the 'asocial' category. The Jews wore the yellow Star of David or a star which was a combination of a yellow and a red triangle which was really used for Jewish political prisoners. Additionally, there were several other symbols for categories of prisoners. The political prisoners came from most of the occupied and annexed countries, so they needed further identification markers. The German political prisoners kept the plain red triangles. The others had letters signifying their nationality put on the triangles. The Norwegians had a black 'N' placed in the middle of the red triangle.

Rahm, Karl

Commandant of Theresienstadt from February 1944 to May 1945. Sentenced to death by a Czechoslovakian court in 1947.

Ravensbrück

Concentration camp for women, located about 90 kilometres north of Berlin. Building started in 1938 on the order of Heinrich Himmler, head of the SS, and the camp opened in May 1939. Of the over 130,000 women and about 20,000 men who were prisoners in Ravensbrück, about 40,000 survived. Women were deported to this camp from all German-occupied countries in Europe, including Norway.

Rosh Hashanah

The Jewish New Year, which begins on the first day of Tishrei (September-October) and lasts for two days. There are ten days between Rosh Hashanah and Yom Kippúr, the Day of Atonement.

Sabbath

Also 'Shabbat'. In Jewish tradition the last of the days of the week, lasting from sunset on Friday to after sunset on Saturday. The word comes from the Hebrew schabbath ('cessation', 'rest'), cf. Exodus 20:8–10 and Deuteronomy 5:12–15. The Sabbath is a day of rest and the most important holy day of Judaism, as it is a weekly event.

Schächter, Rafael

Jewish composer, pianist, and conductor who played a key part in the cultural life of Theresienstadt. In October 1944 he was deported to Auschwitz, where he died.

Schönberg, Arnold

Austrian composer, particularly known for his twelve-tone technique and for his experiments with atonal music.

Scurvy

A disease resulting from vitamin C deficiency which causes fatigue, bleeding skin and gums, loss of appetite and weight loss, among other effects.

Sinding, Christian

Norwegian composer.

Smetana, Bedřich

Czech composer and music teacher.

Sobibór

Extermination camp in the eastern part of Poland. At least 167,000 people were murdered in this camp.

Solicitude

See: 'Introduction'.

SS

Abbreviation of Schutzstaffel, which originally was a bodyguard unit for Hitler and central persons in the NSDAP party. However, the organisation developed into one of the most powerful institutions of the Nazi regime with twelve head offices. Its leader, Heinrich Himmler, had, from 1936, the title Reichsführer-SS und Chef der Deutschen Polizei. From that point in time, the organisation was also the police authority in Germany, which meant that a function which ordinarily is meant to be wielded by the state was transferred to an organisation which at the outset had been a private bodyguard unit. The SS additionally controlled many businesses (for example, Die Deutsche Erd- und Steinwerke GmbH, die Deutsche Ausrüstungswerke GmbH, die Deutsche Versuchsanstalt für Ernährung und Verpflegung GmbH and die Gesellschaft für Textil- und Lederverwertung GmbHH), but its most important functions were the police and the Waffen-SS. The latter consisted of various military formations, including the SS-Totenkopfverbände, who were responsible for guarding the prison camps.

Stadtallendorf

German town about 20 kilometres east of Marburg where, during World War Two, there were forced labour camps attached to large ammunition factories.

Star of David

Six-pointed star formed from two equilateral triangles. The Star of David is an ancient symbol, but was not perceived as a specifically Jewish symbol before the nineteenth century.

Stubova

Prisoner who assisted with the administration of a barracks.

Sub specie aeternitatis

Viewed in an eternal or universal perspective.

Synagogue

Jewish house of worship. The first synagogues probably appeared as early as during the Babylonian Exile in the 6th century BC. During World War Two, Nazi Germany destroyed tens of thousands of synagogues and smaller houses of prayer in Eastern and Central Europe and in the Balkans.

Silence

See: 'Introduction'.

Terezín (Theresienstadt)

See: 'Introduction'.

Tiso, Jozef

Slovakian priest and politician. Head of the German-controlled Slovakian puppet state during World War Two. After the war he was sentenced to death for war crimes.

Torah

The Hebrew name for the Five Books of Moses and the holy writings of the Jews.

Treblinka

Extermination camp in Poland that was situated about 100 kilometres northeast of Warsaw and was in operation from the summer of 1941 to the autumn of 1942. Between 800,000 and 900,000 Jews were murdered in this camp; very few survived.

Trinitrotoluene

Chemical compound best known as TNT. Used as an explosive. TNT is poisonous: handling it causes skin irritations, and prolonged exposure to this substance also has severe negative systemic health effects.

Typhus

A contagious infectious disease that is often transmitted by lice.

Ullmann, Viktor

Jewish composer, conductor, and pianist who made a significant contribution to the cultural activities in Theresienstadt. Was deported to Auschwitz in October 1944 and killed shortly after arrival.

Umschlagplatz

A rounding-up point or trans-shipment place where the Nazis gathered Jews and loaded them onto vehicles, particularly trains, for deportation to concentration and extermination camps.

Verdi, Giuseppe

Italian composer of operas.

Wannsee Conference, The

A conference of senior SS officers and officials in a villa by the lake Wannsee in a suburb of Berlin on 20 January 1942. It was chaired by Reinhard Heydrich, the Chief of the Reichssicherheitshauptamt (RSHA) ('Reich Main Security Office'), and its theme was the extermination of the Jews. The extermination of the European Jews was not decided at this meeting—it was already underway, and those present did not have the mandate to make such a decision—however, it was further planned and organised.

Wehrmacht

The armed forces of Nazi Germany.

Wiesel, Elie

Romanian-born Jewish author, philosopher, and political activist. He survived Auschwitz, and in 1963 he became an American citizen. Awarded the Nobel Peace Prize in 1986. He died in 2016.

White Buses to Auschwitz

Norwegian organisation which arranges documentation trips to the Nazi former concentration camps. See also: 'Bernadotte, Folke'. http://www.hvitebusser.no/omoss

Yom Kippúr

The Jewish Day of Atonement falls on the tenth day of the month Tishrei, which, according to the secular calendar, lasts from 15 September to 14 October.

Zyklon B

Trade name of a German pesticide consisting of hydrogen cyanide (HCN) (also called prussic acid). Used to exterminate prisoners in the Nazi concentration camp gas chambers.

Literature

Assmann, Aleida. 1999. *Erinnerungsräume. Funktionen und Wandlungen des kulturellen Gedächtnisses*. München: C.H. Beck.

Benkow, Jo. 1985. *Fra synagogen til Løvebakken*. Oslo: Gyldendal.

Benkow, Jo. 2012. 'Holocaustdagen 27. januar 2012'
http://www.hlsenteret.no/arrangementer/2912/Jo%20Benkows%20tale%20Holocaustdagen%202012.pdf

Benz, Wolfgang (ed.). 2002. *Lexikon des Holocaust*. München: C.H. Beck.

Benz, Wolfgang, Hermann Graml and Hermann Weiß (ed.). 2001. *Enzyklopädie des Nationalsozialismus*. München: dtv.

Bruland, Bjarte. 2010. 'Deportasjonen og utryddelse av norske jøder'.
http://www.oslo.diplo.de/contentblob/2768328/daten/856867/46_DownloadDatei.pdf

Bruland, Bjarte. 2012. 'Norway's Role in the Holocaust'. In *The Routledge History of the Holocaust*, ed. Jonathan C. Friedman, pp.232-47. London: Routledge.

Børsum, Lise. 2007. *Fange i Ravensbrück*. Oslo: Gyldendal. First published 1946.

Corell, Synne. *Krigens ettertid. Okkupasjonshistorien i norske historiebøker*. Oslo: Spartacus.

Coupechoux, Patrick (ed.). 2003. *Mémoires de déportés: histoires singulières de la déportation*. Paris: La Découverte.

Erll, Astrid. 2011. *Memory in Culture*. Translated by Sara B. Young. New York: Palgrave.

Dahl, Hans Fredrik et al. (ed.). 1995. *Norsk krigsleksikon 1940-45*. Oslo: Cappelen.

Eriksen, Trond Berg, Håkon Harket and Einhart Lorenz. 2005. *Jødehat. Antisemittismens historie fra antikken til i dag*. Oslo: Damm.

Fantlová, Zdenka. 2010. *The Tin Ring*. Newcastle: Northumbria Press. Now published by McNidder & Grace.

Friedman, Jonathan C. (ed.). 2012. *The Routledge History of the Holocaust*. London: Routledge.

Felman, Shoshana and Dori Laub. 1992. *Testimony: Crises of Witnessing in Literature, Psychoanalysis, and History*. NewYork/London: Routledge.

Fure, Odd-Bjørn. 2002. 'Tilintetgjørelsen av de norske jødene'. *Nytt Norsk Tidsskrift* 19:2, pp.111-40.

Goldenberg, Myrna. 2012. 'Double Jeopardy: Being Jewish and Female in the Holocaust'. *The Routledge History of the Holocaust*, ed. Jonathan C. Friedman, pp.389-411. London: Routledge.

Heger, Wanda. 1984. *Hver fredag foran porten*. Oslo: Gyldendal.

Horak, Olga. 2000. *Auschwitz to Australia: A Holocaust Survivor's Memoir*. Sydney: Jagar Sprinting. Now distributed by Sydney Jewish Museum.

LaCapra, Dominick. 1998. *History and Memory after Auschwitz*. Ithaca: Cornell University Press.

Langer, Lawrence L. 1991. *Holocaust Testimony: The Ruins of Memory*. New Haven: Yale University Press.

Laqueur, Walter (ed.). 2001. *The Holocaust Encyclopedia*. New Haven: Yale University Press.

Levin, Irene. 2001. 'Taushetens tale'. *Nytt Norsk Tidsskrift* 18:4, pp.371-82.

Levin, Irene. 2013. 'The Social Phenomenon of Silence'. In *The Holocaust as Active Memory: The Past in the Present*, ed. Marie Louise Seeberg, Irene Levin and Claudia Lenz, pp.187-97. Farnham: Ashgate.

Lorenz, Einhart. 2003. *Veien mot Holocaust*. Oslo: Pax.

Lothe, Jakob. 2016. 'Narrative, Testimony, Fiction: The Challenge of Not Forgetting the Holocaust'. In *Being Contemporary: French Literature, Culture, and Politics Today*, ed. Lia Brozgal and Sara Kippur, pp. 162-76. Liverpool: Liverpool University Press.

Lothe, Jakob and Anette Storeide (ed.). 2006. *Tidsvitner. Fortellinger fra Auschwitz og Sachsenhausen*. Oslo: Gyldendal.

Lothe, Jakob, Susan Rubin Suleiman and James Phelan (ed.). 2012. *After Testimony: The Ethics and Aesthetics of Holocaust Narrative for the Future.* Columbus: Ohio State University Press.

Lothe, Jakob and Jeremy Hawthorn (ed.). 2013. *Narrative Ethics.* New York: Rodopi.

Løgstup, Knud E. 1956. *Den etiske fordring.* København: Gyldendal.

Miller, J. Hillis. 2011. *The Conflagration of Community: Fiction before and after Auschwitz.* Chicago: University of Chicago Press.

Mendelsohn, Oskar. 1987. *Jødenes historie i Norge gjennom 300 år.* Vol.2. Oslo: Universitetsforlaget.

Ottosen, Kristian. 1995. *I slik en natt. Historien om deportasjonen av jøder fra Norge.* Oslo: Aschehoug.

Piper, Franciszek and Teresa Świebocka (ed.). *Auschwitz: Nazi Death Camp.* Oświęcim: The Auschwitz-Birkenau State Museum.

Rees, Laurence. 2005. *Auschwitz: The Nazis & The 'Final Solution'.* London: BBC Books.

Schjølberg, Oddvar. 2006. *Angitt av mamma* [about Maria Gabrielsen]. Risør: Aktive Fredsforlag.

Sebak, Per Kristian. 2008. *'Vi blir neppe nogensinne mange her'.* Jøder i Bergen 1851-1945. Bergen: Vigmostad & Bjørke.

Seeberg, Marie Louise, Irene Levin and Claudia Lenz (ed.). 2013. *The Holocaust as Active Memory: The Past in the Present.* Farnham: Ashgate.

Segal, Maria. 2009. *Maria's Story: Childhood Memories of the Holocaust.* Santa Barbara: Boehm Group.

Stanghelle, Harald. 2004. 'Tidsvitnenes tale'. *Aftenposten*, 31 October.

Storeide, Anette H. 2007. *Fortellingen om fangenskapet.* Oslo: Conflux.

Storeide, Anette H. 2010. *Arven etter Hitler. Tysklands oppgjør med naziregimet.* Oslo: Gyldendal.

Suleiman, Susan Rubin. 2006. *Crises of Memory and the Second World War.* Cambridge, Mass.: Harvard University Press.

Søbye, Espen. 2003. *Kathe, alltid vært i Norge.* Oslo: Oktober.

Tak for alt. The Story of Holocaust Survivor and Civil Rights Activist Judith Meisel. Film produced by Laura Bialis and edited by Broderick Fox. DVD c.60 mins. Sirena Films, Los Angeles, 1998.

United States Holocaust Memorial Museum Encyclopedia of Camps and Ghettos, 1933-1945. http://ushmm.org/research/center/encyclopedia/

Vetlesen, Arne Johan. 2005. *Evil and Human Agency: Understanding Collective Evildoing.* Cambridge: Cambridge University Press.

Volavková, Hana. 1993. ... *I never saw another butterfly ... Children's Drawings and Poems from Terezín Concentration Camp 1942-1944.* New York: Schocken Books.

Vold, Jan Erik. 2007. *Ruth Maiers dagbok. En jødisk flyktning i Norge.* Oslo: Gyldendal.

Young, James E. 1988. *Writing and Rewriting the Holocaust: Narrative and the Consequences of Interpretation.* Indiana: Indiana University Press.

http://jodiskmuseumoslo.no
http://www.hlsenteret.no
http://www.sydneyjewishmuseum.com.au/
http://kaplancentre.uct.ac.za/
http://jewishsantabarbara.org/
http://www.ushmm.org/
http://www.yadvashem.org/
http://en.auschwitz.org/h/index.php
http://www.jewishmuseum.org.pl/en/
http://www.pamatnik-terezin.cz/en?lang=en
http://bergen-belsen.stiftung-ng.de

Index